The *Knox®* *Gelatine* *Cookbook*

A Benjamin Company/Rutledge Book

Color Photographs by Walter Storck

Prepared and Produced by Rutledge Books,
a division of Arcata Consumer Products Corporation.
Published by The Benjamin Company, Inc.
  485 Madison Avenue
  New York, N.Y. 10022
Library of Congress Catalog Card Number: 76-44584
ISBN: 0-87502-050-X
Printed in the United States of America.

Contents

If you can boil water...

... you can get the hang of cooking with Knox Unflavored Gelatine—it's that easy. And one of the great things about Knox cookery is that all those delicious dishes you turn out can be made ahead. Whip them up the night before, in the morning when you're doing the breakfast dishes, at noon when you're fixing lunch for the kids. By dinner time you'll have a mini-masterpiece ready to serve, without any last-minute panic. If you want something in a hurry, Knox can help there, too. Some dishes, such as the Blend 'n Gels, can be whipped up an hour before serving.

Whatever kind of food you have in mind, from a snack to a banquet, Knox is ready to help you make it better than ever. Imaginative appetizers. Softly gelled soups. Creative main dishes that make everyday foods (even leftovers!) seem new and different. Hearty whole-meal salads that satisfy the most demanding appetite. Shimmery salads-on-the-side, savory with vegetables or sweet with fruit. Piquant relishes that add zest to the meal. Wholesome candy gels that kids and grown-ups alike can't leave alone. And as for delicious, tempting desserts—well, you won't believe the variety, from simple to sumptuous, until you really get into cooking with Knox Unflavored Gelatine.

One very important thing to know about Knox Gelatine: it's flavorless, colorless, and sugarless. That means you can flavor as you like, with whatever you like; you can sweeten or not, with sugar or with sugar substitutes. If you're a waistline watcher you'll love it— dishes that are lower in calories taste better when they're made with Knox, which contains only 25 calories per envelope. No preservatives, either. Just plain, unflavored gelatine, ready to help you be the creative cook you've dreamed of being. Use fresh fruits and juices, fresh vegetables, canned and/or frozen fruits and vegetables, fresh eggs and milk and cream, cooked meats and poultry and seafood. And leftovers! Use up a

dib of this and a dab of that to create dishes that look and taste brand new.

How do you get started? First, you learn the basic ways to use unflavored gelatine. There are only a few, and each one of them is simple. Go on from there to try the wonderful recipes in this book and the unflavored gelatine recipes in other cookbooks that you've wondered if you could make successfully. Then let your imagination have full play—try out your own ideas, create your own dishes. It's *easy*, it's fun.

Getting down to basics

Very simple to remember: 1 envelope of unflavored gelatine contains the equivalent gelling strength of one tablespoon of gelatine and will gel 2 cups of liquid. If the recipe you want to use calls for gelatine by the tablespoon, just use one envelope for each tablespoon called for.

Preparation couldn't be simpler: Dissolve the gelatine, combine it with the remaining ingredients, and chill the mixture until firm. There's virtually no cooking involved—instead of *you* standing over a hot stove, the dish made with Knox does the standing, in the refrigerator, while you go about your business. At serving time, bring it straight to the table or stop a moment in the kitchen to unmold and/or garnish it.

7

To get you into the swing of Knox kitchen magic, here are the basic recipes for you to try.

BASIC DESSERT GEL   about 4 servings

1 envelope Knox
 Unflavored Gelatine
2 to 4 tablespoons sugar

2 cups fruit juice or drink,*
 heated to boiling

In a medium bowl, mix unflavored gelatine with sugar. Add boiling liquid; stir until gelatine is completely dissolved. Pour into a 2-cup bowl or individual dessert dishes; chill until firm.

*Do not use fresh or frozen pineapple juice. It contains an enzyme that prevents the mixture from gelling.

Molded Dessert Gel: Decrease liquid by ¼ cup.
Fruited Dessert Gel: Prepare as for Molded Dessert Gel, except chill mixture, stirring occasionally, until it is

the consistency of unbeaten egg whites. Fold in 1½ cups chopped fresh or frozen (except pineapple) or canned fruit; turn into a 3-cup bowl or mold or into individual dessert dishes. Chill until firm.

Fruit Whip: Prepare Basic Dessert Gel mixture. Pour it into a deep mixing bowl. Chill, stirring occasionally, until mixture is almost set and very lumpy. Beat at high speed of electric mixer until very frothy and tripled in volume. Turn into a 6-cup bowl or individual dessert dishes; chill until set. About 8 servings.

BASIC SALAD GEL   about 4 servings

1 **envelope Knox Unflavored Gelatine**
2 **tablespoons sugar**
1½ **cups juice, broth, or water, heated to boiling**

2 **tablespoons vinegar or lemon juice**

In a medium bowl, mix unflavored gelatine with sugar. Add boiling liquid; stir until gelatine is completely dissolved. Stir in vinegar or lemon juice. Pour into a 2-cup bowl or individual dishes; chill until firm.

Molded Salad Gel: Decrease liquid by ¼ cup.
Crunchy Salad Gel: Prepare as for Molded Salad Gel, except chill mixture, stirring occasionally, until it is the consistency of unbeaten egg whites. Fold in 1½ cups cut-up vegetables, cooked meat or fish, or any combination of these. Turn into a 3-cup bowl or mold or individual dishes; chill until firm.

What goes with what?

Almost any food you can think of combines beautifully with unflavored gelatine. Here are some ideas to get you started.

Liquid: Fresh, frozen, or canned fruit juice. Fruit punches, nectars, and ades. Tomato and other vegetable juices or combinations. Broths.

Fruits: Fresh, frozen, or canned peaches, plums, pears, apricots, grapes, cherries. All varieties of berries and melons. Canned pineapple, fruit cocktail.

Vegetables, raw: Finely shredded green or red cabbage, spinach, or carrots. Chopped celery, green pepper, cu-

cumber, or cauliflower. Sliced green onions or radishes.
Vegetables, cooked: Canned, frozen, or cooked fresh cut
green or wax beans, corn, asparagus, lima beans, sliced
carrots, peas, kidney beans, chick peas (garbanzos).
Meat, poultry, fish, shellfish: Diced cooked chicken, ham,
tongue, pork, veal, beef. Flaked cooked fish of any kind.
Flaked canned tuna, salmon. Flaked crab meat. Diced
shrimp or lobster.

That's not the end of course, only the beginning.
Virtually anything you like to eat will combine with
unflavored gelatine into an exciting new-way dish. Feel
free to experiment. You'll enjoy it, and you'll add a
whole new world of dishes to your culinary repertoire,
some simple, some elegant, all good. And all thrifty,
because that's one of the great advantages of unflavored gelatine—it enhances and helps extend the foods
you combine with it, and it has a magic touch with leftovers. And here's a thrifty bonus—don't throw away
flavor, vitamins, and minerals. Use the drained-off juices
of cooked and/or canned or frozen foods that contain
these valuable nutrients as part of the liquid in your gel
dishes. Good, and good for you.

Here are some anything-goes-with-anything combinations for you to try. Then use your inventiveness to go
on from there with new combinations.
Salads: Clear gel with cabbage, carrots, green onions,
radishes. Tomato juice gel with tuna or shrimp, cucumber, green onions, olives. Beef broth gel with ham or
beef, lima beans, cauliflower, radishes, green pepper.
Chicken broth gel with chicken or veal, celery, pimiento,
onion.
Desserts: Orange gel with peaches and strawberries.
Lemon gel with fruit cocktail. Cranberry-juice gel with
oranges and walnuts. Fruit-punch gel with pears and
grapes. Apricot gel with melon balls and blueberries.

Knox know-how
Sometimes you may be somewhat puzzled by a direction
given you in a recipe, particularly one that is a bit more
elaborate than the simple, basic gels. Here's what the
basic directions mean.
"Stir until gelatine is completely dissolved": Use a rubber spatula, stirring constantly and scraping the sides

and bottom of the bowl or pan as you stir. Make sure all the granules of gelatine have vanished before you go on to the next step—if not, the dish you're making won't get firm. But take it easy. Too vigorous stirring will splash granules of gelatine on the sides of the bowl or pan.

"Chill until mixture is the consistency of unbeaten egg whites": This may sound rather vague, but there's no other way to describe the consistency, no way to give a definite time by which this consistency will occur, because chilling time varies with the amount of mixture and the temperature of the refrigerator. As a general rule, it takes the mixture between 20 and 45 minutes to reach this consistency. Why not just skip this step, add the remaining ingredients, and chill until firm? Because chilling to the consistency of unbeaten egg whites ensures the even distribution of the solid ingredients—vegetables, meat, or whatever.

"Chill until mixture mounds slightly when dropped from a spoon": This direction is most often given when beaten egg whites or whipped cream are to be incorporated into the gelatine mixture, in such dishes as chiffons or bavarians. To test, follow the directions—spoon up a little of the chilled mixture and let it slip off the spoon back into the bowl. It should mound or puddle slightly rather than stream off the spoon.

"Fold in": Gently is the key here. Using a rubber spatula or wooden spoon, cut down into the mixture in the center of the bowl, turn the spoon or spatula flat, sweep gently across the bottom, and bring the spatula to the surface of the mixture near the edge of bowl that is closest to you. Give the bowl a quarter turn and repeat, continuing until the gelatine mixture and the other ingredients are well blended. When folding in whipped cream or beaten egg whites, be particularly gentle—otherwise, you'll lose some of the air trapped in the whipped mixture, and the volume of the finished dish will not be as great, nor the texture as fluffy, as you'd like it to be.

"Chill until firm": You know what firm is, but how long does it take? As with other steps in chilling, this varies, depending on the ingredients used and the temperature of your refrigerator. Individual molds and some

10

pies will be firm in less than 3 hours. A large soufflé or other large gel may take 4 to 6 hours, or overnight. To be on the safe side, make a dish that will serve a large number the day before the party. Not only does this ensure a perfectly firmed product, but it also makes life easier on party day!

"Turn into a mold or individual serving dishes": Molds lend flair to party tables—a fish-shaped mold of salmon mousse, for example, can be the hit of the buffet both in looks and taste. Tall molds of shimmering gel are very handsome. For family meals, individual dishes or any size kitchen bowl can be used. Try unusual containers, too—tea cups, demitasse cups, brandy snifters, parfait glasses, or shells of fruit or vegetables, such as oranges, grapefruit, tomatoes, or green peppers.

"Unmold to serve": To many cooks, this is the scary part. Take courage, it's easy when you know how. Dip the mold into warm (not hot) water to the depth of the gelatine contents for about 5 seconds. (Keep an eye on the clock, or count as kids do: one raccoon, two raccoons, and so on.) Remove it from the water. Carefully loosen the gel from the sides of the container with the tip of a sharp, thin-bladed knife. Tilt or shake the container gently to loosen the gel. Invert a serving dish on top of the container. Hold the container and the serving dish firmly together and turn both over. Shake them gently until the gelatine slips from the container onto the serving dish. If the gel doesn't come out easily, you've probably been too cautious—repeat the process.

"Garnish, if desired": With what? There are plenty of garnishes from which to choose, and you probably have many of the possible ones in your kitchen right now. For desserts, try whipped cream or topping, fresh or cooked or candied fruit, mint or grape leaves, cookie crumbs, crushed hard candy, grated chocolate or chocolate curls, whole or chopped nuts. For salad and main-dish gels, choose salad greens, watercress or parsley sprigs, nasturtium leaves, cucumber slices or fingers, tomato wedges, whole cherry tomatoes, carrot curls, lemon wedges, strips of pimiento, sliced olives. These are merely suggestions, to spark your own creativity. Let your imagination run riot. Almost anything pretty and edible can be used as a garnish.

Spreading your wings

You've been introduced to the nucleus of Knox "cooking," Basic Dessert Gel and Basic Salad Gel. Now it's time to get acquainted with all kinds of other wonderful basic ways of using unflavored gelatine to do you proud.

Whips: Simply, clear gel plus air. The basic gel is chilled until partially set, then beaten until fluffy.

Snows: Clear gel plus egg whites. Basic gel is partially set, unbeaten egg whites are added, and the mixture is beaten until stiff, then chilled until firm. Snows are sometimes called "sponges."

BASIC FRUIT-JUICE SNOW   8 servings

1 envelope Knox
  Unflavored Gelatine
½ cup cold water
½ cup sugar
1 can (6 ounces) frozen fruit
  juice concentrate,
  not thawed*

¾ cup ice water
2 unbeaten egg whites

In a medium saucepan, mix unflavored gelatine with cold water. Let stand 1 minute. Stir over medium heat until gelatine is completely dissolved, about 1 minute; remove from heat. Stir in sugar, frozen concentrate, and ice water; stir until concentrate melts. Chill, if necessary, until slightly lumpy.

Place egg whites in a chilled bowl; add gelatine mixture. Beat at high speed of electric mixer until mixture begins to hold its shape, about 7 minutes. Spoon into a 6-cup bowl or individual dessert dishes; chill until firm. If desired, serve with fruit or custard sauce.

*Use frozen orange or grape concentrate, lemonade, limeade, or any fruit punch—except pineapple. (Fresh or frozen pineapple will not gel.)

Chiffons: These are custard gels to which beaten egg whites are added. Egg yolks are cooked with the gelatine to make a custard base. Chiffons make fine desserts as they are, or they can be used for light, airy pie fillings—excellent in baked pastry shells or cracker or cookie-crumb crusts.

BASIC VANILLA CHIFFON   6 servings

1 envelope Knox Unflavored Gelatine	1¾ cups cold milk, divided
6 tablespoons sugar, divided	2 eggs, separated
	1½ teaspoons vanilla extract

In a medium saucepan, combine unflavored gelatine, 2 tablespoons sugar, and ½ cup cold milk. Let stand 1 minute. Beat egg yolks with remaining 1¼ cups milk; stir into gelatine mixture. Stir over low heat until gelatine is completely dissolved, about 5 minutes. Remove from heat, stir in vanilla. Chill, stirring occasionally, until mixture mounds slightly when dropped from a spoon.

In a medium bowl, beat egg whites until soft peaks form. Gradually add remaining 4 tablespoons sugar and beat until stiff. Fold gelatine mixture into beaten egg whites. Turn into a 4-cup bowl or mold or into individual dishes. Chill until set.

Chocolate Chiffon: Mix ¼ cup unsweetened cocoa with the gelatine, sugar, and milk.

Coffee Chiffon: Mix 2 tablespoons regular instant coffee powder with the gelatine, sugar, and milk. Substitute ½ teaspoon almond extract for the vanilla.

Lemon Chiffon: Substitute 2 teaspoons grated lemon peel and 2 tablespoons lemon juice for the vanilla.

Peppermint Chiffon: Substitute ¼ teaspoon peppermint extract for the vanilla; if desired, add a few drops red food coloring.

Mousses and bavarians: A mousse is a clear gel, chilled to the consistency of unbeaten egg whites, at which point whipped cream is added. A bavarian is a custard gel (made with egg yolks) with both beaten egg whites and whipped cream added—the richest, most delectable member of the gel family. There are no basic approaches to either of these. There are both sweet and savory mousses—raspberry mousse, curried chicken mousse, salmon mousse, to name a few. Bavarians, on the other hand, are almost always desserts, served with fruit or other sweet sauces, with whipped cream, or both.

Mousses and bavarians—and chiffons, as well—can be served in a number of ways, dressed up for their final chilling. An orange chiffon, for example, turned into a chocolate cookie-crumb crust and decorated with chocolate curls, makes a delicious and beautiful pie you'll be proud to serve. Or turn any chiffon, mousse, or bavarian mixture into a serving dish or springform pan lined with ladyfingers. Presto—you've produced a superb charlotte.

There are some recipes throughout this book for wonderful pies, soufflés, charlottes, and other elegant dishes that will make you look like a master cook. Most of them are relatively simple to prepare, all have the immeasurable advantage of being make-aheads, with no last-minute hassle. That's the great thing about Knox —when you're cooking for company, you can enjoy your own party; when you're making a meal for the family, you can spend dinner time with them instead of at the stove.

Blend 'n Gel, the sudden, simple masterpiece: When you have drop-in guests, to whom you say impulsively, "Do stay for supper!" before you remember you have no dessert prepared, or when you've planned an informal evening and intended to stop at the bakery on the way home but forgot—for any dessert-in-a-hurry, turn to Blend 'n Gel. The technique offers even more. If you'd like to make your family's favorite molded salad tonight, but the idea of all that chopping and cutting up turns you off, turn to Blend 'n Gel. Your blender will do the work for you. The technique is simple, and the entire process—from start to gel—is fast.

BASIC VANILLA BLEND 'N GEL   6 to 8 servings

2 envelopes Knox Unflavored Gelatine	2 eggs
1½ cups cold milk, divided	⅓ cup sugar
1 cup milk, heated to boiling	2 teaspoons vanilla extract
	1 cup ice cubes (about 6 to 8)

In a 5-cup blender container, sprinkle unflavored gelatine over ½ cup cold milk. Let stand 3 to 4 minutes. Add boiling milk; cover and process at low speed 2 minutes. Add remaining 1 cup cold milk, eggs, sugar, and vanilla. Add ice cubes, one at a time, and process at high speed until ice is melted.

Pour into individual serving dishes; chill until set, about 30 minutes.

Idea: If you want a richer dessert, use ½ cup cold milk and 1 cup cold heavy cream in place of the cold milk.

Chocolate Blend 'n Gel: Add 1 package (6 ounces) semi-sweet chocolate pieces at the same time as the eggs and sugar. Reduce the vanilla extract to 1 teaspoon.

Mocha Blend 'n Gel: Prepare Chocolate Blend 'n Gel, adding 1 tablespoon instant coffee powder with the chocolate pieces.

Strawberry Blend 'n Gel: Add 1 package (10 ounces) frozen strawberries, partially thawed, and 2 teaspoons lemon juice at the same time as the eggs and sugar. Omit the vanilla extract.

Orange Blend 'n Gel: Add the grated peel and chopped fruit of one orange at the same time as eggs and sugar. Omit the vanilla extract. 15

A cinch to make (but not as fast-setting as the Blend 'n Gel desserts) is this up-to-date version of an old family favorite.

BLEND 'N GEL COLESLAW   8 servings

2 envelopes Knox Unflavored Gelatine	1 cup mayonnaise
	1 medium onion, quartered
½ cup cold water	2 cups cabbage pieces
1 cup boiling water	1 cup celery pieces
1 teaspoon salt	1 cup peeled cucumber
2 tablespoons lemon juice	pieces

In a 5-cup blender container, sprinkle unflavored gelatine over cold water. Let stand 3 to 4 minutes. Add boiling water; cover and process at low speed 2 minutes. Add salt, lemon juice, and mayonnaise; process until well blended. Stop blender and add onion; process at high speed until finely chopped. Stop blender and add cabbage, celery, and cucumber pieces; cover and process at high speed only until coarsely chopped.

Turn into a 6-cup bowl and chill until firm, 2 to 3 hours.

Knox Blox*—new-style snack treat for everybody: Neat little squares of jewel-like gelatine, shimmery clear or crammed with goodies—don't they sound delicious? They are because they're Knox Blox, a new and different way with unflavored gelatine that's become a favorite with everyone from eight to eighty. They're finger-firm gelatine squares that you can eat with your fingers. They don't melt at room temperature, so you can keep 'em out for quick snacking.

They couldn't be easier to make! The basic recipe calls for Knox Unflavored Gelatine, boiling water, and your favorite flavorings—but there are all sorts of variations, including two lower calorie versions that are veritable dieter's delights. In every case, it's the amount of Knox you use that makes these squares firm enough for finger snacking.

Beginning on page 17, you'll find a whole collection of recipes for these unusual little finger foods—sweet ones and savory—that you'll like to make, that your family and friends will like to make disappear.

16

Cooking for two?

Often it's more difficult to put together a menu for two than one for twenty, because a cook is limited by the fact that most recipes yield quantities for four or six.

Let Knox help you add variety and pleasure to your meals. Choose recipes that yield four servings, and turn the finished product into four individual molds or serving dishes. Bring two to the table tonight, reserve two —covered, in the refrigerator—to serve tomorrow or the day after. You'll find, in this book, a great variety of delicious dishes to suit your small-family needs—soups, main dishes, salads, desserts. There's a wide new cooking-for-two world waiting for you.

Now that you're familiar with the basic Knox cooking techniques and recipes, try the whole repertoire of unflavored gelatine dishes, simple to fancy, light to rich, in the pages that follow. Enjoy!

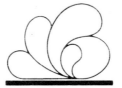

The great American snack-time revolution

Candy, crackers, cookies, chips, pretzels, nuts —each has had its day. But now there's new Knox Blox that everyone's making, everyone's eating. (Bloxing is becoming a big thing, and in time it may sweep the other snacks off the boards.) What are these nifty newfangled munchers? They're finger food, as good snacks ought to be, firmed-up little gelatine squares that won't melt, even at room temperature. What do they taste like? That's another of their charms—they'll accommodatingly take on any flavor you want them to. They can be simple, fruit-flavored squares. They can be nutty, chocolatey, creamy, coconutty, fudgy, butterscotchy. And if a sweet snack isn't what you crave, try savory Knox Blox that are salady, seafoody, chickeny, tomatoey. By the time you've tried them all, you'll have the hang of it and want to create new versions of your own, with your own favorite ingredients, your own bestliked flavors. You'll be making them for in-front-of-television munching, for neighbors who drop in, for buffet dinners, for desserts—for everything. They're fun.

KNOX FRUITED BLOX   about 100 squares

4 envelopes Knox
    Unflavored Gelatine
2 packages (3 ounces each)
    fruit-flavored gelatine

4 cups boiling water
1 can (17 ounces) fruit
    cocktail, undrained

In a large bowl, combine unflavored gelatine and flavored gelatine. Add boiling water and stir until gelatine is completely dissolved. Stir in fruit cocktail. Pour into a shallow baking pan, about 9 x 13 inches; chill until firm. To serve, cut into 1-inch squares.

Another way: *Substitute 1 can (20 ounces) crushed pineapple, undrained, or 1 can (16 ounces) sliced peaches, undrained and chopped, for the fruit cocktail.*

TROPICAL KNOX BLOX   about 80 squares

Be sure to use canned, not fresh or frozen, pineapple juice in these—the fresh or frozen juice will keep them from getting firm, disappointing anxiously waiting snackers

4 envelopes Knox
    Unflavored Gelatine
⅓ cup sugar
2 cups canned pineapple
    juice, heated to boiling

1 teaspoon rum extract
    (optional)
⅓ cup flaked coconut

In a medium bowl, mix unflavored gelatine with sugar. Add boiling juice and stir until gelatine is completely dissolved. Stir in rum extract. Pour into a 9-inch-square pan; sprinkle with coconut. Chill until firm. To serve, cut into 1-inch squares.

SUNNY CITRUS BLOX   60 to 80 squares

These fruity and light treats are only 5 calories per square

4 envelopes Knox
    Unflavored Gelatine
¾ cup canned unsweetened
    grapefruit or pine-
    apple juice

1 cup boiling water
Artificial sweetener to equal
    ¼ cup sugar
1 cup orange juice

In a medium bowl, mix unflavored gelatine with grapefruit juice. Add boiling water and stir until gelatine is completely dissolved. Stir in artificial sweetener and orange juice. Pour into an 8- or 9-inch-square pan and chill until firm. To serve, cut into 1-inch squares.

"ORANGE-YOU-GLAD" BLOX

about 100 squares

7 envelopes Knox
   Unflavored Gelatine
⅓ cup sugar
3 cups boiling water
1 can (6 ounces) frozen
   orange juice concen-
   trate

2 cans (11 ounces each)
   mandarin oranges,
   undrained
½ cup white crème de
   cacao

In a large bowl, mix unflavored gelatine with sugar. Add boiling water and stir until gelatine is completely dissolved. Add remaining ingredients and stir until concentrate is melted and mixture is well blended. Pour into a shallow baking pan, about 9 x 13 inches; chill until firm. To serve, cut into 1-inch squares.

19

APRICOT BLOX

about 80 squares

3 envelopes Knox
   Unflavored Gelatine
1 package (3 ounces)
   orange-pineapple- or
   orange-flavored
   gelatine

1 cup apricot nectar
1½ cups boiling water
½ cup dried apricots
¼ cup apricot brandy
   (optional)

In a 5-cup blender container, sprinkle unflavored gelatine and flavored gelatine over nectar; let stand 3 to 4 minutes. Add boiling water and process at low speed 2 minutes; add apricots and brandy and process at high speed until apricots are puréed, about 2 minutes. Pour into a 9-inch-square pan; chill until firm. To serve, cut into 1-inch squares.

HAPPY APPLE BLOX

about 80 squares

Newfangled way to eat an apple a day, plus a delicious, crunchy bonus topping of walnuts

4 envelopes Knox Unflavored Gelatine	2½ cups apple juice, heated to boiling
¼ cup sugar	¾ cup chopped walnuts

In a medium bowl, mix unflavored gelatine with sugar. Add boiling apple juice and stir until gelatine is completely dissolved. Pour into a 9-inch-square pan; sprinkle with walnuts. Chill until firm. To serve, cut into 1-inch squares.

Other ways: *For the walnuts, substitute seedless raisins or flaked coconut—or use a combination of two, or all three.*

SPICED APPLE BLOX

60 to 80 squares

Sweet and spicy, these tasty blox are only 5 calories per square

20

4 envelopes Knox Unflavored Gelatine	Artificial sweetener to equal ¼ cup sugar
2 cups unsweetened applesauce, divided	¼ teaspoon ground cinnamon
¾ cup boiling water	⅛ teaspoon ground nutmeg

In a medium bowl, mix unflavored gelatine with ½ cup applesauce. Add boiling water and stir until gelatine is completely dissolved. Stir in artificial sweetener, cinnamon, nutmeg, and remaining 1½ cups applesauce. Pour into an 8- or 9-inch-square pan and chill until firm. To serve, cut into 1-inch squares.

BANANA SPLIT BLOX

about 80 squares

4 envelopes Knox Unflavored Gelatine, divided	2 medium bananas, thinly sliced
1 package (3 ounces) strawberry-flavored gelatine	¼ cup sugar
	1 cup (½ pint) vanilla ice cream, softened (or heavy cream)
2½ cups boiling water, divided	Topping (suggestions follow)

Strawberry layer: In a large bowl, combine 2 envelopes

unflavored gelatine and the flavored gelatine. Add 1½ cups boiling water and stir until gelatine is completely dissolved. Stir in bananas. Pour into a 9-inch-square pan; chill until almost set.

Cream layer: In a large bowl, mix 2 envelopes unflavored gelatine with the sugar. Add 1 cup boiling water and stir until gelatine is completely dissolved. Stir in ice cream until melted. Carefully pour onto strawberry layer. Sprinkle with desired topping; chill until firm. To serve, cut into 1-inch squares.

Suggested toppings: chopped maraschino cherries or nuts, chocolate sprinkles, miniature marshmallows.

"OLD GLORY" BLOX   about 100 squares

6 envelopes Knox
  Unflavored Gelatine,
  divided
10 tablespoons sugar,
  divided
3½ cups boiling water,
  divided
1 can (15 ounces)
  blueberries in light
  syrup, undrained

1 cup (8 ounces) plain
  yogurt
1 package (10 ounces)
  frozen raspberries in
  syrup, thawed

Blue layer: In a large bowl, mix 2 envelopes unflavored gelatine with 4 tablespoons sugar. Add 1 cup boiling water and stir until gelatine is completely dissolved. Stir in blueberries. Pour into a shallow baking pan, about 9 x 13 inches; chill until almost set.

White layer: In a large bowl, mix 2 envelopes unflavored gelatine with 2 tablespoons sugar. Add 1 cup boiling water and stir until gelatine is completely dissolved. With wire whip or rotary beater, blend in yogurt. Carefully pour onto blue layer; chill until almost set.

Red layer: In a large bowl, mix 2 envelopes unflavored gelatine with 4 tablespoons sugar. Add 1½ cups boiling water and stir until gelatine is completely dissolved. Stir in raspberries. Carefully pour onto white layer; chill until firm. To serve, cut into 1-inch squares.

GRASSHOPPER GRABS   about 100 squares

6 envelopes Knox
   Unflavored Gelatine,
   divided
1 package (3 ounces) lime-
   flavored gelatine
¼ cup sugar
3 cups boiling water,
   divided

⅓ cup green crème de
   menthe
3 cups (1½ pints) vanilla
   ice cream, softened,
   divided
1 package (4½ ounces)
   chocolate instant
   pudding mix

Mint layer: In a large bowl, combine 4 envelopes unflavored gelatine, the flavored gelatine, and sugar. Add 2 cups boiling water and stir until gelatine is completely dissolved. Stir in crème de menthe and 2 cups ice cream until melted. Pour into a shallow baking pan, about 9 x 13 inches; chill until almost set.

Chocolate layer: In a large bowl, mix 2 envelopes unflavored gelatine with the pudding mix. Add 1 cup boiling water and stir until gelatine is completely dissolved. Stir in 1 cup ice cream until melted. Carefully pour onto mint layer; chill until firm. To serve, cut into 1-inch squares.

23

BLOX OF FUDGE   60 to 80 squares

4 envelopes Knox
   Unflavored Gelatine
½ cup sugar
1½ cups boiling water

1 package (12 ounces)
   semisweet chocolate
   pieces

In a medium saucepan, mix unflavored gelatine with sugar. Add boiling water and stir until gelatine is completely dissolved. Add chocolate pieces; stir with wire whip over low heat until chocolate is melted and thoroughly blended, about 5 minutes. Pour into an 8- or 9-inch-square pan; chill until firm. To serve cut into 1-inch squares.

Other ways: *For Rocky Road Blox, stir in ½ cup each chopped nuts and marshmallow creme before pouring into pan; for Cherry Fudge Blox, stir in ½ cup chopped maraschino cherries.*

KNOX DOUBLE-DECKER BLOX

about 100 squares

(Illustration page 22)

4 envelopes Knox
Unflavored Gelatine
3 packages (3 ounces each)
flavored gelatine

3 cups boiling water
1 cup (½ pint) heavy
cream

In a large bowl, combine unflavored gelatine and flavored gelatine. Add boiling water and stir until gelatine is completely dissolved. Add cream; stir well. Pour into a shallow baking pan, about 9 x 13 inches; chill until firm. To serve, cut into 1-inch squares.

BLACK FOREST BLOX

about 100 squares

Here's the cherry-chocolate combination of Vienna's famous Black Forest Cake captured in these good little chewy dessert snacks

3 envelopes Knox
Unflavored Gelatine
3 packages (3 ounces each)
cherry-flavored gelatine

4 cups boiling water
1 package (6 ounces)
semisweet chocolate
pieces

In a large bowl, combine unflavored gelatine and flavored gelatine. Add boiling water and stir until gelatine is completely dissolved. Pour into a shallow baking pan, about 9 x 13 inches. Sprinkle with chocolate pieces. Chill until firm. To serve, cut into 1-inch squares.

PUDDING KNOX BLOX

about 80 squares

5 envelopes Knox
Unflavored Gelatine
1 package (3½ ounces)
vanilla instant pudding
mix

1½ cups boiling water
1½ cups cold milk

In a large bowl, mix unflavored gelatine with pudding mix. Add boiling water and beat with wire whip or rotary beater until well blended. Stir in milk. Pour into a 9-inch-square pan; chill until firm. To serve, cut into 1-inch squares.

Other ways: *Any favorite flavor instant pudding mix can be used in this recipe—lemon, chocolate, banana cream, coconut cream. To make Toffee Crunch Blox: use butterscotch instant pudding mix; chill until firm. Melt 1 package (6 ounces) semisweet chocolate pieces with 2 tablespoons water. Dribble over surface of Blox. Sprinkle with ½ cup chopped walnuts or pecans. Chill until chocolate is firm.*

JUST FANCY-GOOD BLOX about 80 squares

5 envelopes Knox
   Unflavored Gelatine
1 cup chocolate-flavored
   syrup

1 cup boiling water
1 cup marshmallow creme
1 cup chunky peanut butter

In a large saucepan, sprinkle unflavored gelatine over syrup. Add boiling water and stir until gelatine is completely dissolved. Add marshmallow creme and peanut butter; stir over low heat until marshmallow creme is melted, about 5 minutes. Pour into a 9-inch-square pan; chill until firm. To serve, cut into 1-inch squares.

25

PECAN DANDIES about 100 squares

7 envelopes Knox
   Unflavored Gelatine
¾ cup brown sugar
3 cups apple juice, heated
   to boiling

1 cup (½ pint) heavy cream
1 cup finely chopped pecans
1 teaspoon ground
   cinnamon
1 teaspoon vanilla extract

In a large bowl, mix unflavored gelatine with sugar. Add hot apple juice and stir until gelatine is completely dissolved. Stir in remaining ingredients. Pour into a shallow baking pan, about 9 x 13 inches; chill until firm. To serve, cut into 1-inch squares.

BLOX-BUSTERS

about 80 squares

5 envelopes Knox
  Unflavored Gelatine
¾ cup cold water
2 cups vegetable juice
  cocktail or tomato
  juice, heated to boiling

2 tablespoons sugar
½ teaspoon salt
2 cups finely chopped
  vegetables (sugges-
  tions follow)
Few drops hot pepper sauce

In a large bowl, mix unflavored gelatine with water. Add hot vegetable juice and stir until gelatine is completely dissolved; stir in remaining ingredients. Pour into a 9-inch-square pan; chill until firm. To serve, cut into 1-inch squares.

Suggested vegetables: carrots, celery, cucumber, green pepper, mushrooms, radishes, green onions, zucchini.

SALAD BLOX

about 80 squares

2 envelopes Knox
  Unflavored Gelatine
1 package (3 ounces)
  lime-flavored gelatine
1½ cups boiling water

2 cups (16 ounces) creamed
  cottage cheese
½ cup coarsely chopped
  walnuts
½ cup seedless raisins

In a large bowl, combine unflavored gelatine and flavored gelatine. Add boiling water and stir until gelatine is completely dissolved; cool. Stir in cottage cheese and pour into a 9-inch-square pan. Sprinkle with walnuts and raisins; chill until firm. To serve, cut into 1-inch squares.

Other ways: *For Pineapple Salad Blox, add 1 can (8¼ ounces) crushed pineapple; for Apple Salad Blox, add 3 medium apples, finely chopped.*

NUTTY SALAD BLOX

about 80 squares

4 envelopes Knox
  Unflavored Gelatine
⅓ cup sugar
2 cups cranberry juice
  cocktail, heated to
  boiling

1 cup orange juice
1 medium orange, finely
  chopped
½ cup thinly sliced celery
¼ cup chopped walnuts

In a large bowl, mix unflavored gelatine with sugar. Add hot cranberry juice and stir until gelatine is completely dissolved. Stir in remaining ingredients. Pour into a 9-inch-square pan; chill until firm. To serve, cut into 1-inch squares.

Another way: *For Apple Berry Salad Blox, substitute an additional 1 cup cranberry juice for the orange juice, and 1 apple, chopped, for the orange.*

CRAB LOUIS EN BLOX   about 100 squares

6 envelopes Knox
   Unflavored Gelatine
¼ cup sugar
2½ cups boiling water
1 cup mayonnaise
½ cup Wish-Bone® Deluxe
   French or Thousand
   Island Dressing

½ cup chili sauce
2 cups flaked cooked
   crab meat
½ cup chopped celery
1 hard-cooked egg,
   chopped (optional)

In a large bowl, mix unflavored gelatine with sugar. Add boiling water and stir until gelatine is completely dissolved. With wire whip or rotary beater, blend in remaining ingredients. Pour into a shallow baking pan, about 9 x 13 inches; chill until firm. To serve, cut into 1-inch squares.

SALMON "LOX BLOX"   about 80 squares

4 envelopes Knox
   Unflavored Gelatine
¾ cup cold water
1¼ cups boiling water
1 cup (8 ounces) dairy
   sour cream
¾ cup Wish-Bone Thou-
   sand Island Dressing

2 teaspoons lemon juice
1 can (7¾ ounces) salmon,
   drained and flaked
3 tablespoons finely
   chopped onion

In a large bowl, mix unflavored gelatine with cold water. Add boiling water and stir until gelatine is completely dissolved. With wire whip or rotary beater, blend in remaining ingredients. Pour into a 9-inch-square pan; chill until firm. To serve, cut into 1-inch squares.

CHICKEN 'N CURRY BLOX

about 100 squares

Here's a brand-new kind of appetizer that will set your guests humming—great flavor, and they'll keep their easy-eat shape all evening, but they'll be gobbled up in no time!

5 envelopes Knox Unflavored Gelatine
2 packages (3 ounces each) lemon-flavored gelatine
3 envelopes instant chicken flavor broth
3 cups boiling water

1½ cups mayonnaise
1½ cups diced cooked chicken
¾ cup chopped celery
2 tablespoons finely chopped onion
1¼ teaspoons curry powder

In a large bowl, combine unflavored gelatine, flavored gelatine, and broth powder. Add boiling water and stir until gelatine is completely dissolved. With wire whip or rotary beater, blend in remaining ingredients. Pour into a shallow baking pan, about 9 x 13 inches; chill until firm. To serve, cut into 1-inch squares.

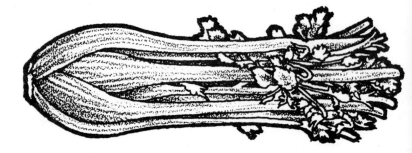

Off to a good start

When you have appetizers in mind, Knox Unflavored Gelatine can help you like an extra pair of hands in the kitchen. Whether you have invited a few people in for drinks and snacks or have planned a big, smashing buffet spread, Knox's magnificent make-aheads ease your work load, because they not only look and taste great, but they're finished and ready to serve hours before your guests arrive. You can bring unflavored gelatine appetizers to the table in triumph—creamy gelled spreads, piquant pâtés, handsome rings with extra goodies piled high in their centers. On different occasions, you might want to offer serve-on-a-plate, eat-with-a-fork appetizers or tangy, gently gelled soup to begin the meal. Knox can help you with these, too. If you have in mind the West Coast way to start a meal, with salad, you'll find some here and more in the Salads Ready to Serve section. Finally, if you need more ideas, turn to page 18, where there are lots of great new Knox Blox recipes, many just right for the appetizer table. With the help of Knox, you can really have fun at your own party.

For the cocktail hour, the buffet table

Here are savory snacks, nibbles, spreads, molds, pâtés to do you proud, to make your party a winner. All are delicious with flavors *you* choose, ingredients *you* decide on, because unflavored gelatine lets you make them that way. There's no sugar or flavoring to clash with the natural tastes of the foods you choose.

THOUSAND ISLAND SALMON SPREAD

about 5 cups

2 envelopes Knox
  Unflavored Gelatine
½ cup cold water
1 cup boiling water
2 cups (16 ounces) dairy
  sour cream

¾ cup Wish-Bone Thousand
  Island Dressing
1 tablespoon lemon juice
1 can (16 ounces) salmon,
  drained and flaked
1 teaspoon dill weed

31

In a medium bowl, mix unflavored gelatine with ½ cup cold water. Add 1 cup boiling water and stir until gelatine is completely dissolved. Add sour cream, dressing, lemon juice, salmon, and dill weed. Turn into a 5½-cup mold and chill until firm, about 4 hours.

SHRIMP PATE

about 3½ cups

1 envelope Knox
  Unflavored Gelatine
¼ cup lemon juice
¼ cup cold water
2 cups (16 ounces) dairy
  sour cream
¾ cup chili sauce

2 tablespoons prepared
  horseradish
½ pound shrimp, cleaned,
  cooked, and finely
  chopped (about 1½
  cups)

In a medium saucepan, mix unflavored gelatine with lemon juice and water; let stand 1 minute. Stir over medium heat until gelatine is completely dissolved, about 1 minute. Remove from heat; cool. Blend in sour cream, chili sauce, and horseradish; fold in shrimp. Turn into a 3½-cup mold or loaf pan; chill until firm. Unmold onto a serving plate. Garnish with parsley and green olives, if desired.

PARTY LIVER-WALNUT PATE about 3 cups

Easy to make, looks great, tastes even better—what more could you ask of a savory mold elegant enough to grace an elaborate buffet?

1 envelope Knox
   Unflavored Gelatine
1 can (about 13 ounces)
   consommé madrilene
2 hard-cooked eggs, shelled
   and cut up
2 cans (4¾ ounces each)
   liver spread

½ cup chopped walnuts
1 tablespoon sweet-pickle
   relish, drained
½ teaspoon salt
¼ teaspoon pepper

In a medium saucepan, mix unflavored gelatine with madrilene; let stand 1 minute. Stir over medium heat until gelatine is completely dissolved, about 1 minute.

Into a 3-cup bowl, pour a layer of gelatine mixture about ½ inch deep. Refrigerate until almost firm, about 15 minutes. Cool remaining gelatine mixture at room temperature.

Through a sieve, force hard-cooked eggs over gelatine mixture remaining in saucepan. Add remaining ingredients and beat until well blended. Pour over gelatine layer in bowl. Chill until firm, about 4 hours or overnight. Unmold onto a serving plate. If desired, garnish top of pâté with sliced olives and surround with crisp crackers.

DEVILED HAM AND EGG PATE about 4 cups

2 envelopes Knox
   Unflavored Gelatine
2 envelopes instant beef
   flavor broth
3 cups cold water
3 cans (4½ ounces each)
   deviled ham

½ cup sweet-pickle relish
1 tablespoon prepared
   mustard
4 hard-cooked eggs, finely
   chopped

In a medium saucepan, mix unflavored gelatine with broth powder. Add water; let stand 1 minute. Stir over medium heat until gelatine and broth are completely dissolved, about 4 minutes. Chill, stirring occasionally, until mixture is the consistency of unbeaten egg whites.

Blend in thoroughly ham, sweet-pickle relish, and mustard. Fold in eggs. Turn into a 6-cup mold or loaf pan; chill until firm. Unmold onto a serving plate.

Idea: *To make this pâté party pretty, decorate the top or surround the mold or both with one or a combination of these garnishes: sliced hard-cooked egg, sliced stuffed olives, pimiento strips, crumbled bacon, parsley sprigs.*

DOUBLE-CHEESE APPETIZER about 4 cups

Zesty blue and mellow cream cheeses pair perfectly in this tasty mold—serve with pumpernickel party bread or, even better, celery chunks and apple slices

2 **envelopes Knox Unflavored Gelatine**	½ **cup crumbled blue cheese**
1 **cup cold water**	¼ **cup chopped parsley**
1 **cup (½ pint) light cream**	¾ **teaspoon onion salt**
2 **packages (8 ounces each) cream cheese, softened**	1 **teaspoon worcestershire sauce**

In a medium saucepan, mix unflavored gelatine with water; let stand 1 minute. Stir over medium heat until gelatine is completely dissolved, about 1 minute. Remove from heat; stir in cream.

In a medium bowl, blend cream cheese with blue cheese. Stir in parsley, onion salt, and worcestershire; gradually blend in gelatine mixture. Turn into a deep 4-cup bowl or mold; chill until firm. Unmold onto a serving plate. Garnish with parsley sprigs, if desired.

SHRIMPLY DELICIOUS COCKTAIL RING

12 servings

2 envelopes Knox
  Unflavored Gelatine
1 cup cold water
1½ cups tomato juice,
  heated to boiling
1 cup chili sauce
¼ cup lemon juice
2 to 3 tablespoons
  prepared horseradish

⅛ teaspoon hot pepper
  sauce
½ cup chopped celery
½ cup chopped green
  pepper
2 pounds shrimp, cleaned,
  cooked, and chilled

In a medium bowl, mix unflavored gelatine with water. Add hot tomato juice and stir until gelatine is completely dissolved. Add chili sauce, lemon juice, horseradish, and hot pepper sauce; chill, stirring occasionally, until mixture is the consistency of unbeaten egg whites.

Fold in celery and green pepper. Turn into a 6-cup ring mold; chill until firm, about 4 hours. To serve, unmold onto a serving plate, fill center with shrimp.

GUACAMOLD

about 6 cups

As pleasing to the eye as to the palate, this provocatively flavored avocado appetizer is almost—but not quite!—too pretty to be eaten

2 envelopes Knox
  Unflavored Gelatine
1 cup cold water
4 cups mashed avocado
  (about 4 medium
  avocados)
1 cup (8 ounces) dairy
  sour cream

2 teaspoons salt
1½ tablespoons grated
  onion
2 tablespoons lemon juice
2 teaspoons chili powder
Corn chips or crisp crackers

In a medium saucepan, mix unflavored gelatine with water. Let stand 1 minute. Stir over medium heat until gelatine is completely dissolved, about 1 minute. Remove from heat; cool. Combine avocado and sour cream; stir in remaining ingredients. Blend in gelatine mixture. Turn into a 6-cup mold; chill until firm. Unmold onto a serving plate and serve with chips or crackers.

Special ways to start a meal

To get sit-down meals off to a flying start, here are flavorful appetizers and softgel soups with the natural taste of your own good ingredients. With Knox know-how to guide you, you'll learn the secret of easy perfection in no time.

JEWEL CONSOMME

4 servings

Inviting way to start a meal—cups of shimmery softgel consommé, beef or chicken flavored, tangy with lemon

1 envelope Knox Unflavored Gelatine
3 envelopes instant beef or chicken flavor broth
½ cup cold water
1¾ cups boiling water
2 tablespoons lemon juice
Garnishes (suggestions follow)

In a medium bowl, mix unflavored gelatine and broth powder with cold water; let stand 1 minute. Add boiling water and stir until gelatine and broth are completely dissolved. Stir in lemon juice. Chill until softly set, about 3 hours. To serve, spoon into cups; garnish as desired.

Garnishes: If you like, top each serving with one of the following: snipped parsley, chives, or watercress; a dollop of unsweetened whipped cream or dairy sour cream; packaged croutons or broken pretzel sticks; sliced green onions; sieved hard-cooked egg; finely chopped green pepper, celery, or cucumber.

Another way: *For the boiling water, substitute 1¾ cups tomato juice, heated to boiling.*

BEST-EVER BORSCHT

6 servings

Rosy, shimmery, invitingly cool-looking—who would guess that each serving "costs" only 40 calories?

1 envelope Knox
   Unflavored Gelatine
	1 can (15 or 16 ounces)
	   diced beets, undrained

2 envelopes instant beef
   flavor broth
	4 teaspoons prepared
	   horseradish

1½ cups cold water	1 tablespoon lemon juice

In a medium saucepan, mix unflavored gelatine with broth powder. Add water; let stand 1 minute. Stir over medium heat until gelatine and broth are completely dissolved, about 4 minutes. In a medium bowl, combine beets and their liquid, horseradish, and lemon juice. Stir in hot gelatine mixture; chill until thickened. (Mixture will not become firm, but rather achieve a thick-but-not-stiff consistency, called softgel, that is just right for gelatine-based soups.) Serve in chilled cups. Garnish with celery seed, if desired.

SPRINGTIME PEA SOUP

5 to 6 servings

1 envelope Knox Unflavored Gelatine	1 tablespoon grated onion
½ cup cold water	½ teaspoon salt
2 envelopes instant chicken flavor broth	¼ teaspoon white pepper
1½ cups boiling water	⅛ teaspoon ground cardamom (optional)

1 package (10 ounces)
   frozen peas
	1 cup (½ pint) light or
	   heavy cream

In a 5-cup blender container, sprinkle unflavored gelatine over cold water; let stand 3 to 4 minutes. Add broth powder and boiling water; cover and blend 1 minute at low speed. Add peas, onion, salt, pepper, and cardamom. Blend at medium speed 2 minutes, or until peas are puréed. Add cream; process 1 minute.

Pour into a medium bowl; chill until set, about 3 hours. Spoon into cups to serve. If desired, garnish with croutons or mint leaves.

Note: *This soup will not become firm, but will have a softgel set, the proper consistency for a gelled soup. In* *case you're wondering, no cooking is required, not even for the peas!*

SHRIMP COCKTAIL BITES   8 servings

Get the meal off to a flying start with these hearty and satisfying shrimp-tomato mouthfuls—only 100 calories a serving

4 envelopes Knox Unflavored Gelatine	**1½ tablespoons prepared horseradish**
2 tablespoons sugar	**1 tablespoon lemon juice**
½ teaspoon salt	
1½ cups boiling water	**1½ cups chopped cooked shrimp**
2 cups tomato juice	
½ cup Wish-Bone Low-Calorie Russian Dressing	**1 cup finely chopped green pepper**

In a medium bowl, combine unflavored gelatine, sugar, and salt. Add boiling water and stir until gelatine is completely dissolved. Stir in tomato juice, Russian dressing, horseradish, and lemon juice.

Pour into a shallow baking pan, about 9 x 13 inches. Sprinkle with shrimp and green pepper. Chill until firm, about 3 hours. To serve, cut into bite-size squares. If desired, arrange on lettuce-lined plates and garnish with lemon wedges.

ZESTY SEAFOOD APPETIZER   6 servings

2 envelopes Knox Unflavored Gelatine	**3 tablespoons lemon juice**
½ cup cold water	**1 tablespoon prepared horseradish**
2 cups clamato juice, heated to boiling	**1 can (8 ounces) minced clams, drained**
¼ cup chili sauce	

In a medium bowl, mix unflavored gelatine with water. Add clamato juice and stir until gelatine is completely dissolved. Stir in chili sauce, lemon juice, and horseradish. Chill, stirring occasionally, until mixture is the consistency of unbeaten egg whites.

Fold in clams. Turn into individual ½-cup molds; chill until firm. Unmold onto lettuce-lined plates.

CHILLY CHEESE PIE

12 servings

This appetizer is also delicious cut in thin wedges and served as a snack or with cocktails

2 envelopes Knox
  Unflavored Gelatine
½ cup cold milk
1 cup milk, heated to
  boiling
6 ounces roquefort or blue
  cheese, mashed
¼ cup lemon juice
¼ cup chopped parsley

¼ cup diced pimiento
2 teaspoons grated onion
½ teaspoon salt
¼ teaspoon hot pepper
  sauce
1½ cups (¾ pint) heavy
  cream, whipped
1 baked 9-inch pastry
  shell

In a medium bowl, mix gelatine with cold milk. Add boiling milk and stir until gelatine is completely dissolved. Cool. Add cheese and lemon juice; beat with rotary beater until smooth. Stir in parsley, pimiento, onion, salt, and hot pepper sauce. Chill, stirring occasionally, until mixture is the consistency of unbeaten egg whites.

Fold in whipped cream. Pile into pastry shell. Chill until firm. Cut in wedges to serve.

39

A LITTLE BIT OF ITALY

20 servings

4 envelopes Knox
  Unflavored Gelatine
3½ cups cold water,
  divided
2 cups boiling water
1½ cups Wish-Bone
  Italian Dressing
1½ cups chopped green
  pepper

½ cup sliced pitted ripe
  olives
⅓ cup diced pimiento
1 can (7 ounces) tuna,
  drained and flaked
1 can (4 ounces) sliced
  mushrooms, drained

In a large bowl, mix unflavored gelatine and ½ cup cold water. Add 2 cups boiling water and stir until gelatine is completely dissolved. Add remaining 3 cups cold water and Italian dressing; chill, stirring occasionally, until mixture is the consistency of unbeaten egg whites.

Fold in green pepper, olives, pimiento, tuna, and mushrooms. Turn into a 13- x 9- x 2-inch pan or individual molds and chill until firm. To serve, cut into squares and place each serving on a lettuce leaf. Garnish with ripe olives, salami, and provolone cheese, if desired.

Main dishes
that wait

When your menu calls for a main dish made with unflavored gelatine, you're way ahead of the game. Such dishes can be put together in the morning—even the night before, if you prefer—and are ready to serve when you are. When you want a quick-but-good dinner for the family on a busy day, when you've invited a crowd for a buffet spread, when you'd like to serve lunch or supper outdoors without any last-minute fuss, call in Knox. With these hearty, satisfying, great-flavor main dishes, you'll have time on your hands at the end of the day. Time isn't all you'll be saving either—gelatine main dishes for the family are economical, too. For parties, they're tried-and-proved crowd-pleasers that look handsome, taste wonderful. In an eye-appealing mold, you can serve meat, fish, or poultry in a savory, shimmery mixture that has great appetite-appeal, too. Make plenty. Everybody's going to be coming back for seconds when you serve a Knox main dish.

Thrifty family favorites

Some family main dishes are inexpensive, but not all that great. Some are wonderful, but not all that budget-minded. These are both, thanks to the magic of unflavored gelatine—and they're quick 'n easy besides!

Cooking-for-two note: turn into individual molds or serving dishes, refrigerate the extra portions to make a triumphant second appearance at dinner the day after tomorrow.

HAM AND POTATO MEDLEY   8 servings

Two old favorites get together in this tasty make-ahead main dish, just right for a summer supper on the patio

2 envelopes Knox
   Unflavored Gelatine
1 cup cold water
1 envelope instant onion
   soup
3 tablespoons vinegar
1 cup milk
1 cup mayonnaise
2 tablespoons prepared
   horseradish

1½ cups finely diced
   cooked potato
   (2 medium potatoes)
1 cup finely chopped
   ham
1 cup chopped celery
¼ cup chopped green
   pepper

In a medium saucepan, mix gelatine with cold water. Let stand 1 minute. Stir over medium heat until gelatine is completely dissolved, about 1 minute. Remove from heat; stir in instant soup and vinegar. Gradually add milk to mayonnaise, stirring until smooth. Stir in gelatine mixture and horseradish. Add remaining ingredients. Mix well. Turn into a 6-cup mold. Chill until firm. Unmold to serve. Garnish with hard-cooked eggs and cherry tomatoes, if desired.

Great go-alongs: *Serve with sweet-sour wilted cucumbers, old-fashioned mixed mustard pickles, whole wheat bread and butter, spice cake (make it in the cool of the morning) with lemon sauce, and iced tea.*

CLAM/TOMATO RING

6 servings

Here's a tangy main-dish mold that's low in calories, high in flavor—including the cottage cheese, it contains only about 140 calories per serving

1 can (10¼ ounces)
   minced clams
2 envelopes Knox
   Unflavored Gelatine
½ cup cold water
1 teaspoon worcestershire
   sauce

2¾ cups tomato juice
1 cup thinly sliced celery
¼ cup sliced green onions
2 cups (16 ounces) lowfat
   cottage cheese
2 tablespoons snipped
   chives

Drain clams, reserving liquid. In a medium bowl, mix unflavored gelatine and cold water. To reserved clam liquid, add enough water to make ¾ cup; add worcestershire sauce. Heat to boiling; pour over gelatine and stir until gelatine is completely dissolved. Stir in tomato juice. Chill, stirring occasionally, until mixture is the consistency of unbeaten egg whites.

Stir in clams, celery, and green onions. Turn into a 5-cup ring mold. Chill until firm. Combine cottage cheese and chives. To serve, unmold gelatine ring, fill center with cottage cheese.

Great go-alongs: *Start the meal with cups of hot instant beef flavor broth. With the main dish serve cole slaw, dill pickle strips, crisp melba toast. For dessert, ice milk or wedges of chilled cantaloupe. Add tea, hot or cold, for the grown-ups and skim milk for the children, or diet soft drinks all around, and the whole family will have a tasty and satisfying low-calorie supper*

Other ways: *Omit cottage cheese and chives, fill center of the unmolded ring with chilled cooked green beans, broccoli, or cauliflower, lightly dressed with bottled low-calorie Italian dressing. For a flavor change, substitute canned vegetable juice cocktail for the tomato juice. Another time, instead of tomato juice use 2¾ cups of hot instant chicken flavor broth; cool before stirring into gelatine mixture.*

NEW-DAY GAZPACHO

4 servings

Gazpacho takes on substance in this family favorite—and there are only 40 calories in each substantial serving

1 envelope Knox Unflavored Gelatine	⅛ teaspoon hot pepper sauce
½ cup cold water	2 tablespoons chopped onion
1 envelope instant beef flavor broth	¼ cup finely chopped celery
¾ cup boiling water	½ cup finely chopped green pepper
¼ cup vinegar	1½ cups chopped fresh tomatoes
½ teaspoon salt	
1 teaspoon paprika	
½ teaspoon dried basil	

In a medium bowl, mix unflavored gelatine with cold water. Let stand 1 minute. Sprinkle broth powder over gelatine mixture. Add boiling water and stir until gelatine and broth are completely dissolved. Stir in vinegar, salt, paprika, basil, and hot pepper sauce. Chill, stirring occasionally, until mixture is the consistency of unbeaten egg whites.

43

Fold in remaining ingredients. Turn into individual cups or molds. Chill until firm. Unmold—on lettuce leaves, if desired.

Great go-alongs: *For a completely delicious light supper, serve with deviled eggs (moisten yolks with bottled low-calorie Italian dressing), lowfat cottage cheese, crisp rye wafers, carrot curls, and cucumber fingers. Fresh fruit for dessert, skim milk or iced tea to drink.*

PANTRY-SHELF SUPPER

6 servings

2 envelopes Knox
   Unflavored Gelatine
½ cup cold water
2 envelopes instant beef
   flavor broth
2 cups boiling water
½ cup Wish-Bone Creamy
   Garlic or California
   Onion Dressing

1 can (12 ounces) luncheon
   meat, cubed
1 cup diced swiss cheese
1 cup diced peeled apple

In a medium bowl, mix unflavored gelatine with cold water. Let stand 1 minute. Sprinkle broth powder over gelatine mixture. Add boiling water and stir until gelatine and broth are completely dissolved. Cool. Stir in dressing. Chill, stirring occasionally, until mixture is the consistency of unbeaten egg whites.

Fold in remaining ingredients. Turn into a 6-cup mold; chill until firm. Unmold to serve.

44

Great go-alongs: *Serve with thick-sliced tomatoes sprinkled with salt, pepper, and dried basil, hot whole wheat rolls. For dessert, lemon pie—homemade, frozen, or from the bakery. Tea for adults, milk for the children.*

CREAMY TUNA SALAD

4 servings

1 envelope Knox
   Unflavored Gelatine
¼ cup cold water
2 envelopes instant
   chicken flavor broth
1¼ cups boiling water
1 teaspoon lemon juice
⅓ cup mayonnaise

¼ small onion
1 stalk celery, cut into
   1-inch pieces
3 pimiento-stuffed olives
   (optional)
1 can (6½ or 7 ounces)
   tuna, drained

In a 5-cup blender container, sprinkle unflavored gelatine over cold water; let stand 3 to 4 minutes. Add broth powder and boiling water; cover and process at low speed until gelatine and broth are completely dissolved. Add remaining ingredients; cover and process at high speed just until vegetables are chopped.

Turn into a 3- or 4-cup mold. Chill until firm. Unmold to serve.

Great go-alongs: *For family supper, serve with hot corn bread (from a mix, if you like), pickled beets, and sliced oranges topped with brown sugar and a dab of dairy sour cream.*

DEVILISH EGG TREAT   4 to 6 servings

1 envelope Knox Unflavored Gelatine	¼ teaspoon hot pepper sauce
¼ cup cold water	¼ cup green pepper pieces
½ cup boiling water	1 cup celery pieces
½ cup mayonnaise	4 hard-cooked eggs, quartered
¾ teaspoon salt	

In a 5-cup blender container, sprinkle gelatine over cold water; let stand 3 to 4 minutes. Add boiling water, cover and process at low speed until gelatine is completely dissolved. Add mayonnaise, salt, and hot pepper sauce; cover and process until smooth. Add remaining ingredients, cover and chop by quickly turning on and off at high speed several times.

45

Turn into a 3-cup mold or bowl; chill until set. Garnish with tomato wedges and salad greens, if desired.

Great go-alongs: *For a quick/easy supper, serve this with mugs of cream of tomato soup, a platter of assorted cheeses, crusty bread; add a hearty fruit dessert, such as apple or blueberry pie.*

Especially for company

When the main dish for a company meal can be made ahead, that's half the battle. When it's made with Knox, that's the other half. Real natural flavor—there's nothing artificial about an unflavored gelatine main dish, no unwanted sweetness, nothing to disguise your own good ingredients. Choose one of these delightful dishes to be the star of your next party menu.

PARSLIED HAM   8 to 10 servings

Here is an easy version of jambon persillé, *a molded entrée that graces French cold tables—a perfectly delicious highlight for your summer buffet*

2 envelopes Knox
   Unflavored Gelatine
¾ cup cold white wine
4 envelopes instant
   chicken flavor broth
1 bay leaf
½ teaspoon black pepper
2 tablespoons minced onion

½ teaspoon dried thyme
2¾ cups water
2 tablespoons lemon
   juice
5 cups cubed cooked ham
1 cup finely chopped
   parsley

In a medium bowl, mix unflavored gelatine with cold wine. In a medium saucepan, mix broth powder, bay leaf, pepper, onion, and thyme with water. Simmer 10 minutes; bring to a boil. Strain onto gelatine mixture and stir until gelatine is completely dissolved. Stir in lemon juice. Chill, stirring occasionally, until mixture is the consistency of unbeaten egg whites.

Combine ham and parsley; mix well. Fold into gelatine mixture. Turn into a 2-quart mold or loaf pan; chill until firm. Unmold to serve. Garnish with additional parsley sprigs, if desired.

Great go-alongs: *For a sauce to serve with this superb dish, combine 1½ cups mayonnaise with 3 tablespoons dijon-style mustard; stir in 1 cup chopped mixed candied*

46

fruit. Accompany with hot garlic bread, sautéed corn, and tossed green salad with tomatoes and peanut halves; for dessert, serve an airy Sabayon Snow with Custard Sauce (page 84).

EGGS IN ASPIC   8 servings

Offer luncheon guests these elegant French oeufs en gelée— individual sparkling gelatine molds with a wonderful flavor surprise in their centers

2 envelopes Knox Unflavored Gelatine	2 teaspoons dried tarragon
3¾ cups water, divided	8 cold poached eggs
4 envelopes instant beef flavor broth	1½ cups diced cooked tongue or ham
¼ cup sliced green onions	

In a medium bowl, mix unflavored gelatine with ¾ cup cold water. In a medium saucepan, mix broth powder, green onions, and tarragon with remaining 3 cups water. Simmer 10 minutes; bring to a boil. Strain onto gelatine mixture and stir until gelatine is completely dissolved.

Place 1 tablespoon gelatine mixture in the bottom of each of 8 individual molds. Chill until set, about 10 minutes. Reserve remaining gelatine mixture at room temperature.

Place one poached egg in each mold, surround with diced tongue. Add 2 tablespoons liquid gelatine mixture to each mold; chill 10 minutes.

Fill molds with remaining gelatine mixture. Chill until firm. Unmold to serve.

Great go-alongs: *Garnish with watercress. To complete the meal, finger sandwiches of parsley butter on white bread, chive butter on whole wheat; tossed green salad with cheese cubes and orange sections; pears—home poached, or from a can—with vanilla ice cream and chocolate sauce (Poire Hélène).*

SEASIDE SALAD

16 servings

Chunks of tasty seafood in a tomato-juice gel spiked with lemon and horseradish make a zesty main dish your guests will welcome

6 **envelopes Knox Unflavored Gelatine**	⅓ **cup prepared horseradish**
6 **cups tomato juice, divided**	3 **cups mayonnaise**
⅔ **cup lemon juice**	6 **cups cooked seafood (shrimp, crab meat, or lobster)**
1½ **teaspoons salt**	
1 **tablespoon worcestershire sauce**	3 **cups chopped celery**

In a medium saucepan, mix unflavored gelatine with 3 cups tomato juice. Let stand 1 minute. Stir over medium heat until gelatine is completely dissolved, about 5 minutes. Remove from heat; stir in remaining 3 cups tomato juice, lemon juice, salt, worcestershire, horseradish, and mayonnaise. Beat until smooth. Chill, stirring occasionally, until mixture mounds slightly when dropped from a spoon.

Fold in seafood and celery. Turn into two 8-cup molds; chill until firm. Unmold to serve. Garnish with salad greens, if desired.

Great go-alongs: *For a company-coming meal, start with cups of cream of mushroom soup. With the main dish, serve hot garlic bread, cold cooked asparagus dressed with Wish-Bone Italian Dressing. For dessert, minted fruit compote topped with lime sherbet, and a nice hot beverage. If you like, serve chilled white wine with the meal.*

Another way: *If you'd like to serve a company-good main dish that is very easy on your food budget, substitute flaked solid-pack white tuna for the shellfish in this recipe. Even more economical—and still very good indeed—is chunk-pack light tuna. Whichever you choose, be sure to drain the tuna well before measuring.*

CRANBERRY/CRAB CROWN

6 to 8 servings

Here's a party spectacular—a richly rosy gelatine ring, its center heaped with a savory crab-and-fruit salad topped with crunchy almonds

3 envelopes Knox
  Unflavored Gelatine
1 cup cold water
4 cups cranberry juice
  cocktail, divided
¼ cup sugar
1 tablespoon lemon juice
Fruited Crab Salad
  (recipe follows)
¼ cup toasted slivered
  almonds

In a medium bowl, mix unflavored gelatine with cold water. Heat 2 cups cranberry juice to boiling; add to gelatine and stir until gelatine is completely dissolved. Add sugar and stir until dissolved. Stir in remaining 2 cups cranberry juice and lemon juice. Turn into a 5-cup ring mold; chill until firm. Unmold ring and mound Fruited Crab Salad in center; sprinkle with almonds. Garnish with salad greens or watercress, if desired.

FRUITED CRAB SALAD

3½ cups cooked crab meat
 ½ cup chopped celery
 1 cup halved, pitted bing
    cherries
⅔ cup mayonnaise
1 tablespoon lemon juice
¼ teaspoon ground ginger

Combine crab, celery, and cherries. Blend mayonnaise, lemon juice, and ginger. Add to crab mixture and toss lightly to mix well. Chill until serving time.

Great go-alongs: *Serve hot biscuits, cooked frozen artichoke hearts dressed lightly with Wish-Bone Chunky Blue Cheese Dressing. For dessert, coconut cake with lemon filling. If you wish, offer a chilled rosé wine with the meal.*

Other ways: *Shrimp, tuna, or chicken may be substituted for the crab meat, cut-up peeled oranges or whole green seedless grapes for the cherries.*

CURRIED CHICKEN MOUSSE 12 servings

3 envelopes Knox
  Unflavored Gelatine
3 envelopes instant
  chicken flavor broth
1¼ cups milk
3 eggs, separated
¼ teaspoon salt
1½ teaspoons curry powder
4 cups (2 pounds)
  creamed cottage
  cheese

3 tablespoons lemon juice
4 cups finely chopped
  cooked chicken
⅓ cup finely chopped
  chutney
⅓ cup finely chopped
  pimiento
2 tablespoons minced
  onion
2 cups (1 pint) heavy
  cream, whipped

In a medium saucepan, combine unflavored gelatine, broth powder, and milk. Let stand 3 to 4 minutes. Add egg yolks; mix well. Stir over low heat until gelatine and broth are completely dissolved and mixture thickens slightly, 6 to 8 minutes. Remove from heat; stir in salt and curry powder.

50 Sieve cottage cheese, or beat at high speed of electric mixer until smooth; stir in gelatine mixture. Stir in lemon juice, chicken, chutney, pimiento, and onion. Chill, stirring occasionally, until mixture mounds slightly when dropped from a spoon.

Beat egg whites until stiff but not dry; fold gelatine mixture into egg whites. Fold in whipped cream. Turn into a 12-cup mold; chill until firm. Unmold to serve. If desired, surround with salad greens.

Great go-alongs: *Serve with hot rolls, halved cherry tomatoes and thin-sliced raw zucchini lightly tossed with Wish-Bone Caesar Dressing. For dessert, angel food cake sauced with strawberries or raspberries.*

Another way: *Substitute cold cooked turkey for the chicken in this recipe—a great way to use up turkey leftovers. Cold cooked ham can also be substituted for the chicken, or use a combination of half ham and half chicken or turkey. Veal can also be used. So can lamb, the flavor of which is quite good in this versatile curry-spiced dish.*

APPLE-CURRIED CHICKEN 10 to 12 servings

Here is a truly superb dish to serve (with pardonable pride) to guests—chicken spiced with curry, crunchy with apples and celery and cashew nuts, in a lemon-spiked sour-cream gel

3 envelopes Knox Unflavored Gelatine	3 tablespoons lemon juice 1 tablespoon curry powder
½ cup cold water	2 cups diced cooked
3 envelopes instant chicken flavor broth	chicken 1½ cups diced apple
2 cups boiling water	½ cup thinly sliced celery

2 cups (16 ounces) dairy
   sour cream
	½ cup coarsely chopped
	   salted cashews

1 cup milk	¼ cup finely chopped onion

In a medium bowl, mix unflavored gelatine with cold water. Let stand 1 minute. Sprinkle broth powder over gelatine mixture. Add boiling water and stir until gelatine and broth are completely dissolved. Blend in sour cream, milk, lemon juice, and curry powder. Chill, stirring occasionally, until mixture is the consistency of unbeaten egg whites.

Fold in remaining ingredients. Turn into an 8-cup mold; chill until firm. Unmold to serve. Garnish with parsley or watercress sprigs, if desired.

Great go-alongs: *To complement this curry dish, serve chutney, brown rice salad, wilted cucumbers, thin crisp whole wheat wafers, and a light, fruity dessert, such as Fresh Lemon Snow (page 79). Tea, hot or iced, completes the meal.*

SALMON/GRAPE LOAF 8 to 10 servings

1 can (1 pound) salmon	1 teaspoon salt
3 envelopes Knox Unflavored Gelatine	1 cup chopped celery 1 cup halved seedless
3 envelopes instant chicken flavor broth	green grapes ½ cup finely chopped,
3 cups boiling water	pared, and seeded
2 cups (16 ounces) dairy sour cream	cucumber 2 tablespoons finely
¼ cup cider vinegar	chopped onion

Drain salmon, reserving liquid. To salmon liquid, add

enough water to make ½ cup. Place in a medium bowl and add unflavored gelatine. Sprinkle broth powder over gelatine; add boiling water and stir until gelatine and broth are completely dissolved. Cool. With wire whip or rotary beater, blend in sour cream, vinegar, and salt. Chill, stirring occasionally, until mixture is the consistency of unbeaten egg whites.

Flake salmon and fold into mixture together with remaining ingredients. Turn into a 9- x 5-inch loaf pan; chill until firm. Unmold to serve. Garnish with small grape clusters, if desired.

Great go-alongs: *For a superb summer luncheon, start the meal with cups of vichyssoise (from a can, if you like). With the salmon mold, serve parsley-butter finger sandwiches. To finish the meal, slices of chocolate pound cake topped with orange ice. Iced tea or chilled white wine with the meal.*

FRESH AS SPRING SALAD about 6 servings

2 envelopes Knox Unflavored Gelatine
2 tablespoons sugar
1½ cups boiling water
1 cup mayonnaise
¼ cup Wish-Bone Italian Dressing
3 tablespoons lemon juice
1½ cups chopped cooked asparagus
1 cup chopped cooked shrimp
½ cup chopped tomato
1½ tablespoons finely chopped onion

In a medium bowl, mix unflavored gelatine with sugar. Add boiling water and stir until gelatine is completely dissolved. With wire whip or rotary beater, blend in mayonnaise, Italian dressing, and lemon juice. Chill, stirring occasionally, until mixture is the consistency of unbeaten egg whites.

Fold in remaining ingredients. Turn mixture into a 9-inch layer cake pan and chill until firm, about 4 hours. Unmold to serve. Garnish with tomato wedges, if desired.

Great go-alongs: *Make this the focal point of a company luncheon, served with hot consommé, cucumber sandwiches on thin whole wheat bread; iced tea to drink and raspberry sherbet and macaroons for dessert.*

SUMMER FRUIT SALAD ROSE 6 servings

Only 60 calories per serving for this refreshing, cool, tastes-like-summer fruit-and-wine salad

1 **envelope Knox**	1 **cup thinly sliced peaches**
Unflavored Gelatine	½ **cup thinly sliced banana**
1 **cup water, divided**	½ **cup sliced strawberries**
1¼ **cups rosé wine**	

In a medium saucepan, mix unflavored gelatine with ½ cup water. Let stand 1 minute. Stir over medium heat until gelatine is completely dissolved, about 1 minute. Remove from heat. Add remaining ½ cup water and the wine. Chill, stirring occasionally, until mixture is the consistency of unbeaten egg whites.

Fold in peaches, banana, and strawberries. Turn into 6 individual serving dishes; chill until set.

Great go-alongs: *For a company luncheon that will not do your guests' waistlines any harm, start with Mushroom Broth (instant beef flavor broth with floating slices of raw mushroom). Accompany each salad with sieved lowfat cottage cheese spiked with lemon juice and topped with a fresh strawberry, accompany with rye melba toast. Iced tea is the beverage, thin-sliced sponge cake the dessert.*

55

Salads
ready to serve

One of the home cook's chief objectives is to capture Nature's enormous bounty in dishes her family enjoys, her guests admire. A cool, refreshing salad with every main meal is one way to accomplish this. Salads are dull? They don't have to be. Salads have a sameness? They needn't. Salads can offer tremendous variety in flavor, in ingredients, even in looks. And many a cook's chief objection to them, that they must be made at the last minute, isn't true either—not when they are unflavored gelatine salads that enfold the freshness of vegetables and fruits in a shimmery gel. Another plus—when that gel is made with Knox Unflavored Gelatine there is nothing artificial about the salad. No sweetness to be compensated for. No taste that has to be masked. Just the good flavor you alone are responsible for —as sweet as you like, as tart as you like, as spicy, as lemony, as vinegary. When you make an unflavored gelatine salad, the flavor is up to you, great taste because it's natural. Isn't that what you want? Isn't that what feeding your family well, your guests well, is all about?

Garden-fresh salads

Tossed green salads are very good. So are mixed vegetable salads. So are fruit salads. But in time their appeal wears thin—often because the cook, anxious to serve her family and friends something not only good but good for them, overdoes the salad routine. That's where Knox steps in with new ideas to make the natural goodness of fresh vegetables and fruits new-way wonderful.

FRESH-IS-BEST SALAD
4 servings

Here's a creamy gel flavored with dill and green onions and lots of tasty, crisp bites of fresh vegetables, and it's weight-conscious, too—80 calories a serving

1 envelope Knox
   Unflavored Gelatine
2 tablespoons sugar
1 cup boiling water
1 cup (8 ounces) plain
   yogurt
1 tablespoon white or cider
   vinegar

1 to 2 tablespoons finely
   chopped green
   onions
½ teaspoon dill weed
Vegetable combinations
   (suggestions follow)

In a medium bowl, mix unflavored gelatine with sugar. Add boiling water and stir until gelatine is completely dissolved. Blend in yogurt, vinegar, green onions, and dill weed. Chill, stirring occasionally, until mixture is the consistency of unbeaten egg whites.

Fold in desired vegetable combination. Turn into individual molds or a 3-cup mold; chill until firm. Unmold to serve.

Vegetable combinations: Choose 1 cup shredded cucumber and ¼ cup shredded radish; or ½ cup *each* chopped cauliflower, green pepper, and tomato; or ½ cup *each* chopped tomato, fresh mushrooms, and cooked fresh green beans.

GARDEN SALAD

8 servings

As colorful as it is delicious, this fresh-vegetable salad comes in at only 72 calories a portion—and if you use a sugar substitute, at only 30 calories

2 **envelopes Knox Unflavored Gelatine**	½ **cup lemon juice**
½ **cup cold water**	½ **cup sliced radishes**
2¼ **cups boiling water**	½ **cup grated carrot**
½ **cup sugar or equivalent artificial sweetener**	2 **cups finely shredded cabbage**
½ **teaspoon salt**	½ **cup diced green pepper**

In a medium bowl, mix unflavored gelatine with cold water. Add boiling water and stir until gelatine is completely dissolved. Add sugar or equivalent and salt; stir until dissolved. Stir in lemon juice. Chill, stirring occasionally, until mixture is the consistency of unbeaten egg whites.

58 Fold in remaining ingredients. Turn into 8 individual molds; chill until firm. Unmold to serve.

GREEN GODDESS CUCUMBER COOLER

8 servings

2 **envelopes Knox Unflavored Gelatine**	½ **teaspoon salt**
1 **cup cold water**	1 **teaspoon dried dill weed**
1½ **cups Wish-Bone Green Goddess Dressing**	3 **cups finely chopped cucumber**
1 **teaspoon instant minced onion**	½ **cup chopped celery**

In a medium saucepan, mix unflavored gelatine with cold water. Let stand 1 minute. Stir over medium heat until gelatine is completely dissolved, about 1 minute. Remove from heat; stir in dressing, onion, salt, and dill weed. Chill, stirring occasionally, until mixture is the consistency of unbeaten egg whites.

Fold in cucumber and celery. Turn into a 5-cup mold that has been lightly brushed with additional dressing. Chill until firm. Unmold to serve. Garnish with salad greens and cherry tomatoes, if desired.

CALIFORNIA SPINACH SALAD   8 servings

Start your meal the West Coast way, with a salad—this one, made with plenty of fresh-and-green garden vegetables, takes its great flavor from California onion dressing

2 envelopes Knox
   Unflavored Gelatine
½ cup cold water
1 cup boiling water
2 tablespoons lemon juice
2 tablespoons sugar
¼ teaspoon salt

1 bottle (8 ounces)
   Wish-Bone California
   Onion Dressing
1½ cups chopped raw
   spinach
1½ cups chopped celery
½ cup sliced radishes

In a medium bowl, mix unflavored gelatine with cold water. Add boiling water and stir until gelatine is completely dissolved. Add lemon juice, sugar, salt, and onion dressing. Chill, stirring occasionally, until mixture is the consistency of unbeaten egg whites.

60 Fold in remaining ingredients. Turn into a 6-cup mold; chill until firm. Unmold to serve. Garnish with escarole and radish roses, if desired.

FRESH VEGETABLE SALAD   8 servings

Russian dressing gives this salad its special taste—and if you use the low-calorie kind, there are only 70 calories in each colorful, flavorful serving

2 envelopes Knox
   Unflavored Gelatine
½ cup cold water
2 cups boiling water
1 bottle (8 ounces) Wish-
   Bone Russian Dressing
   (regular or low-calorie)

1 cup sliced fresh
   mushrooms
1 cup diced cucumber
½ cup sliced celery
2 tablespoons thinly sliced
   green onions

In a medium bowl, mix unflavored gelatine with cold water. Add boiling water and stir until gelatine is completely dissolved. Add Russian dressing; chill, stirring occasionally, until mixture is the consistency of unbeaten egg whites.

Fold in remaining ingredients. Turn into a 5-cup mold; chill until firm. Unmold to serve.

VEGETABLE SALAD ITALIANO

8 servings

You could go far and look hard to find a tastier, crisper salad —Italian dressing is the flavor trick, and if you use the dieter's version, there are only 60 calories a serving

1 small cucumber, diced
12 cherry tomatoes, halved
1 cup diced green pepper
1 cup small cauliflowerets
½ cup Wish-Bone Italian Dressing (regular or low-calorie)

2 envelopes Knox Unflavored Gelatine
½ cup cold water
1½ cups boiling water

In a large bowl, toss vegetables with Italian dressing; marinate in refrigerator overnight.

In a medium bowl, mix unflavored gelatine with cold water. Add boiling water and stir until gelatine is completely dissolved.

Stir gelatine into vegetable mixture. Turn into a 6-cup mold; chill until firm. Unmold to serve.

61

CRUNCHY VEGETABLE POP-UPS

9 to 12 servings

1 can (3 to 4 ounces) chopped mushrooms
2 envelopes Knox Unflavored Gelatine
2 cups boiling water
4 teaspoons sugar
1 teaspoon salt

¾ cup lemon juice
½ cup *each*: finely chopped green pepper, cucumber, and radishes
1 cup *each*: finely chopped cauliflower and celery
Lettuce leaves

Drain mushrooms, reserving liquid. To reserved liquid add enough water to make ½ cup. In a medium bowl, mix liquid with unflavored gelatine. Add boiling water and stir until gelatine is completely dissolved. Stir in sugar, salt, and lemon juice. Chill, stirring occasionally, until mixture is the consistency of unbeaten egg whites.

Fold in mushrooms and fresh vegetables. Turn into two sectioned ice cube trays; chill until firm. Unmold; serve 3 or 4 cubes on individual lettuce-lined salad plates.

Favorite salads made a new way

There's no reason to be bored with salads. Old friends take on new style, new appeal, when they're made the innovative unflavored gelatine way. Let Knox show you how to open up a whole new world of side-dish salads.

NEW-WAY THREE-BEAN SALAD
12 servings

1 package (10 ounces) frozen lima beans, cooked and drained

1 can (15 or 16 ounces) red kidney beans, drained

1 can (16 to 20 ounces) garbanzo beans, drained

¼ cup chopped parsley

¼ teaspoon white pepper

4 tablespoons cider vinegar, divided

2½ teaspoons salt, divided

3 envelopes Knox Unflavored Gelatine

2 teaspoons sugar

½ cup cold water

4 cups boiling water

63

In a large bowl, combine lima beans, kidney beans, and garbanzos. Add parsley, pepper, 3 tablespoons vinegar, and 1½ teaspoons salt. Cover and refrigerate about 2 hours, tossing occasionally.

In a medium bowl, mix unflavored gelatine with sugar and ½ cup cold water. Add 4 cups boiling water and stir until gelatine is completely dissolved. Stir in remaining 1 tablespoon vinegar and 1 teaspoon salt. Chill, stirring occasionally, until mixture is the consistency of unbeaten egg whites.

Fold gelatine mixture into bean mixture. Turn into individual molds or cups; chill until firm. Unmold onto salad greens, if desired.

RED RUSSIAN RING

6 to 8 servings

2 envelopes Knox
Unflavored Gelatine
3 cups tomato juice,
divided
½ cup Wish-Bone Russian
Dressing

1 cup finely chopped
green pepper
½ cup finely chopped
celery

In a large bowl, mix unflavored gelatine with ½ cup cold tomato juice. Heat remaining 2½ cups juice to boiling; add to gelatine mixture and stir until gelatine is completely dissolved. Add Russian dressing. Chill, stirring occasionally, until mixture is the consistency of unbeaten egg whites.

Fold in green pepper and celery. Turn into a 5-cup ring mold or bowl; chill until firm. Unmold to serve.

Great go-alongs: *To turn this side-dish salad into a main-dish delight, fill the center of the ring with an oniony egg-salad mixture. Or dress it up with cooked whole shrimp, and send extra Russian dressing to the table.*

64

COOL 'N CREAMY COLESLAW

10 to 12 servings

2 envelopes Knox
Unflavored Gelatine
2 tablespoons sugar
1¾ cups boiling water
1 teaspoon salt
1 cup mayonnaise

½ cup Wish-Bone
California Onion
Dressing
¼ cup lemon juice
5 cups shredded cabbage
1 cup grated carrots

In a medium bowl, mix unflavored gelatine with sugar. Add boiling water and stir until gelatine is completely dissolved. Cool. Blend in salt, mayonnaise, dressing, and lemon juice. Chill, stirring occasionally, until mixture is the consistency of unbeaten egg whites.

Fold in cabbage and carrots. Turn into a 6-cup mold; chill until firm. Unmold to serve.

Great go-alongs: *This is just right with cold sliced ham. Whip up hot corn bread from a mix, and you have a delicious, satisfying meal. Bring leftover salad to the table the day after tomorrow—it will get a second warm welcome.*

SUPER SUNSHINE SALAD

6 servings

1 envelope Knox
   Unflavored Gelatine
¼ cup cold orange juice
¾ cup boiling orange juice
¼ cup sugar
⅛ teaspoon salt

1 lemon, peeled, quartered,
   and seeded
1 cup carrot pieces
1 can (8½ ounces) crushed
   pineapple or pineapple
   chunks in juice

In a 5-cup blender container, sprinkle unflavored gelatine over cold orange juice; let stand 3 to 4 minutes. Add boiling orange juice; cover and process at low speed until gelatine is completely dissolved. Add sugar, salt, and lemon; process at high speed until lemon is liquefied. Add carrot pieces; cover and chop by turning on and off at high speed several times.

Turn into medium bowl; add pineapple and its juice. Chill, stirring occasionally, until mixture is the consistency of unbeaten egg whites. Turn into a 3-cup mold; chill until firm. Unmold to serve. Garnish with salad greens, if desired.

65

UP-TO-DATE WALDORF SALAD

4 to 6 servings

1 envelope Knox
   Unflavored Gelatine
⅓ cup sugar
1½ cups boiling water
½ teaspoon salt
¼ cup lemon juice

2 cups diced, unpeeled
   tart apple
½ cup chopped celery
¼ cup chopped pecans
   or walnuts

In a medium bowl, mix unflavored gelatine with sugar. Add boiling water and stir until gelatine is completely dissolved. Stir in salt and lemon juice. Chill, stirring occasionally, until mixture is the consistency of unbeaten egg whites.

Fold in apple, celery, and pecans. Turn into a 4-cup mold; chill until firm. Unmold to serve. Garnish with salad greens, if desired.

Another way: *It breaks with tradition, but if you cut the apple to 1¾ cups and add ¼ cup white raisins, a lot of fruit lovers will be pleased.*

CRANBERRY-APPLE WALDORF 8 servings

3 envelopes Knox
   Unflavored Gelatine
⅓ cup sugar
1 cup boiling water
3½ cups cranberry juice
   cocktail

1 cup chopped apple
½ cup chopped celery
⅓ cup chopped walnuts

In a large bowl, mix unflavored gelatine with sugar. Add boiling water and stir until gelatine is completely dissolved. Add cranberry juice; pour into an 8- or 9-inch-square pan and chill until mixture is the consistency of unbeaten egg whites.

Fold in apple, celery, and walnuts. Chill until firm. Unmold to serve.

PEARS IN WINE

8 servings

66

4 envelopes Knox
   Unflavored Gelatine
3½ cups ginger ale, divided
1½ cups boiling water
1½ cups white or rosé wine
4 medium pears, peeled
Lemon juice

⅔ cup crumbled blue
   cheese
¼ cup finely chopped
   walnuts
1 tablespoon thinly sliced
   green onions

In a large bowl, mix unflavored gelatine with 1 cup ginger ale. Add boiling water and stir until gelatine is completely dissolved. Cool. Stir in remaining ginger ale and the wine. Chill, stirring occasionally, until mixture is the consistency of unbeaten egg whites. Turn into 8 individual serving dishes.

Halve pears lengthwise; core. Scoop out a small amount of pulp to form a center well. Brush with lemon juice, place cut side up in gelatine mixture. Chill until set, about 3 hours.

In a small bowl, combine blue cheese, walnuts, and green onions. Just before serving, fill pear centers with cheese mixture.

Another way: *In the filling for the pears, substitute 2 packages (3 ounces each) cream cheese and 1 tablespoon grated orange peel for the blue cheese and green onions.*

Relishes to spark a meal

Here's change-of-pace goodness that will give your meals new character. Whatever your main dish, there's a tangy relish salad to enhance its appeal with natural good flavor you choose yourself, in your own kitchen.

PINEAPPLE RELISH   6 to 8 servings

Just right with pork—and a nice change from applesauce—this good-and-pretty relish makes a fine partner for chicken or turkey, too

2 envelopes Knox Unflavored Gelatine	½ teaspoon salt
½ cup cold water	¼ cup vinegar
1 can (1 pound, 4½ ounces) crushed pineapple in syrup	3 tablespoons lemon juice
	1 cup chopped celery
2 tablespoons sugar	½ cup chopped green pepper
	2 pimientos, diced

In a medium bowl, mix unflavored gelatine with water. Drain syrup from pineapple into a 2-cup measure; add enough water to make 2 cups. Heat to boiling; stir into gelatine mixture until gelatine is completely dissolved. Stir in sugar, salt, vinegar, and lemon juice. Chill, stirring occasionally, until mixture is the consistency of unbeaten egg whites.

Fold in drained pineapple, celery, green pepper, and pimientos. Turn into a 4-cup mold; chill until firm. Unmold to serve.

Another way: *Turn relish into individual molds or cups to chill; unmold onto thick slices of canned cranberry jelly.*

LIME RELISH

6 servings

These flavorful molds are the just-right garnish for a platter of cold fried chicken to be eaten outdoors

1 envelope Knox Unflavored Gelatine	⅛ teaspoon salt
1 cup cold water, divided	1 cup finely chopped celery
1 can (6 ounces) frozen limeade concentrate, thawed	1 cup finely chopped cucumber
	¾ cup finely chopped green pepper

In a medium saucepan, mix unflavored gelatine with ½ cup cold water. Let stand 1 minute. Stir over medium heat until gelatine is completely dissolved, about 1 minute. Remove from heat. Stir in remaining ½ cup water, undiluted limeade concentrate, and salt. Chill, stirring occasionally, until mixture is the consistency of unbeaten egg whites.

Fold in vegetables. Turn into six individual ½-cup molds; chill until firm. Unmold to serve.

68

Another way: *To add extra appetite-appeal and substance, unmold each serving on a slice of tomato or drained canned pineapple.*

GEORGIA PEACH RELISH about 6 servings

1 can (16 ounces) peach halves in heavy syrup	1 cinnamon stick, broken
1 envelope Knox Unflavored Gelatine	½ teaspoon whole cloves
½ cup cold water	¼ cup lemon juice
¼ cup brown sugar	¼ cup seedless raisins
	¾ cup chopped celery
	¼ cup slivered almonds

Drain peaches, reserving syrup, and cut into bite-size pieces. In a medium bowl, mix unflavored gelatine with cold water.

In a small saucepan, combine reserved syrup with enough water to make 1½ cups. Add sugar, cinnamon, and cloves. Simmer 10 minutes; bring to a boil. Strain onto gelatine mixture and stir until gelatine is completely dissolved. Stir in lemon juice and raisins. Chill, stirring occasionally, until mixture is the consistency of unbeaten egg whites.

Fold in peaches, celery, and almonds. Turn into individual molds or a 3-cup mold; chill until firm. Unmold to serve.

Idea: *This spicy relish turns roast duck into even more of a special treat, makes baked stuffed pork chops sing.*

CREAMY GARDEN RELISH about 6 servings

1 envelope Knox
   Unflavored Gelatine
2 tablespoons sugar
¼ teaspoon salt
¾ cup boiling water
1 cup (8 ounces) dairy
   sour cream
2 tablespoons white
   vinegar
1 cup drained shredded
   cucumber
¼ cup shredded radishes
2 tablespoons finely
   chopped green onions

In a medium bowl, combine unflavored gelatine, sugar, and salt. Add boiling water and stir until gelatine is completely dissolved. Blend in sour cream and vinegar. Chill, stirring occasionally, until mixture is the consistency of unbeaten egg whites.

Fold in cucumber, radishes, and green onions. Turn into a 3-cup mold; chill until firm. Unmold to serve.

Idea: *This relish makes a perfect partner for roast veal or veal chops, or let it dress up broiled chopped beef. Good with lamb, too—particularly braised shanks or shoulder chops.*

CALICO CORN RELISH   6 servings

1 can (12 ounces) whole
   kernel corn
1 envelope Knox
   Unflavored Gelatine
1 cup water, divided
3 tablespoons sugar
½ cup white vinegar

2 tablespoons lemon juice
2 drops hot pepper sauce
¼ cup sweet-pickle relish
¼ cup finely chopped
   pimiento
2 tablespoons finely
   chopped onion

Drain corn, reserving liquid. In a medium saucepan, mix unflavored gelatine with ½ cup cold water. Let stand 1 minute. Stir over medium heat until gelatine is completely dissolved, about 1 minute. Remove from heat. Stir in sugar, vinegar, remaining ½ cup water, reserved corn liquid, lemon juice, and hot pepper sauce. Chill, stirring occasionally, until mixture is the consistency of unbeaten egg whites.

Fold in corn, sweet-pickle relish, pimiento, and onion. Turn into a 4-cup mold or individual molds; chill until firm. Unmold to serve.

71

CREAMY CRANBERRY RELISH   8 to 10 servings

2 envelopes Knox
   Unflavored Gelatine
1 cup cold water
1 package (3 ounces) cream
   cheese, softened and
   cut into chunks
2 cups (16 ounces) frozen
   whipped topping, thawed

1 jar (14 ounces)
   cranberry-orange
   relish
1 can (8¼ ounces)
   crushed pineapple,
   drained
½ cup chopped almonds

In a medium saucepan, mix unflavored gelatine with cold water. Let stand 1 minute. Stir over medium heat until gelatine is completely dissolved, about 1 minute.

In a large bowl, thoroughly blend cheese and topping; fold in relish, pineapple, and almonds, then fold in gelatine. Turn into a 5-cup mold; chill until firm. Unmold to serve.

Idea: *Serve this special relish with hot or cold meats. Turkey comes to mind at once, but it's great with ham, too.*

Sweet endings

To a great many people, dessert is what a meal is all about. Dessert is what they've waited for through the main course, the happy culmination of long, eager anticipation. And often, because it's the conclusion, the last thing eaten, dessert is what makes the whole meal memorable. Here is a cook's repertoire of desserts that will linger on the tongue and in the mind long after the last mouthful is devoured. It's not usual to say, "Eat your dessert—it's good for you!" but there's no reason that a treat can't also be wholesome instead of just a helping of empty calories. Fresh fruit, nuts, eggs, milk— these are some of the good things that make these unflavored gelatine desserts more than simply a sweet climax to a meal. Natural flavor and the natural goodness of these foods combine, with the help of Knox, in these delightful sweet endings for any meal you have in mind, from the simplest family dinner to the most elaborate company-coming occasion. And they have something else going for them—every one can be prepared far in advance. Make with pleasure, serve with pride!

Family favorites

"What's for dessert?" is a question many women are called upon to answer 365 days a year, so it's no wonder you're always on the lookout for new and different desserts to serve your family. That's where unflavored gelatine comes to the rescue with all these delectable answers. If you're cooking for two, turn these sweets into individual dishes, serve two at one meal and refrigerate two for tomorrow or the day after.

SUMMER CANTALOUPE COOLER

4 to 6 servings

New-way variation of an old-fashioned flavor, the cantaloupe "sundae"—today's version layers melon balls with a lemony fruit–ice-cream mixture

3 cups chilled cantaloupe
   balls, divided
2 envelopes Knox
   Unflavored Gelatine
1 cup lemonade, heated to
   boiling

¼ cup cold lemonade
1 cup (½ pint) vanilla ice
   cream
1 cup ice cubes (6 to 8)

In a 5-cup blender container, purée ½ cup cantaloupe balls. Sprinkle unflavored gelatine over purée; let stand 3 to 4 minutes. Add hot lemonade; process at low speed 2 minutes. Add cold lemonade, ½ cup cantaloupe balls, and ice cream. Add ice cubes, one at a time, and process at high speed until ice is melted. Let stand until mixture is slightly thickened, about 5 minutes.

In parfait glasses or dessert dishes, layer remaining 2 cups cantaloupe balls and gelatine mixture, ending with cantaloupe balls. Chill until set, about 30 minutes.

Great go-alongs: *This is just the right ending for an August Sunday dinner outdoors. Make oven-fried chicken in the cool of the morning, serve it with corn on the cob and New-Way Three-Bean Salad (page 63). Iced tea and this lovely dessert complete the meal.*

FRUIT-JEWELED MELON

8 servings

2 small cantaloupes, halved and seeded	1¾ cups limeade, heated to boiling
1 envelope Knox Unflavored Gelatine	2 drops green food coloring (optional)
¼ cup sugar	1 cup blueberries

Carefully scoop out cantaloupes, leaving a ¾-inch-thick shell. Drain cantaloupe shells; chill. In a medium bowl, mix unflavored gelatine with sugar. Add hot limeade and stir until gelatine is completely dissolved. Add food coloring. Chill, stirring occasionally, until mixture is the consistency of unbeaten egg whites.

Fold in blueberries. Spoon mixture into prepared cantaloupe shells; chill until firm. To serve, cut into wedges.

Idea: *Reserve the meat of the cantaloupe for fruit salad or cups, or chop it and spoon it over ice cream.*

74

WATERMELON ICE

8 servings

Here's a refresher that's like the color and the flavor of a summer day—serve as is for dessert, or use to dress up fresh fruit cups and salads

6 cups small chunks watermelon, seeded	1 cup sugar
¼ cup lemon juice	1 cup boiling water
2 envelopes Knox Unflavored Gelatine	

Place watermelon, about one quarter at a time, in a 5-cup blender container; cover and process until smooth and liquid. Pour into a large bowl. Stir in lemon juice. In a medium bowl, mix unflavored gelatine with sugar. Add boiling water and stir until gelatine is completely dissolved. Cool slightly; stir into watermelon mixture. Pour mixture into two 9- x 9- x 2-inch pans. Freeze until firm around edges, about 1½ hours.

Spoon into a large bowl; beat until smooth. Return to pans and freeze until firm, 3 to 4 hours.

CHOCOLATE CHIP MINT DESSERT

about 6 servings

2 envelopes Knox
  Unflavored Gelatine
½ cup cold milk
1 cup very hot milk
1 cup (½ pint) heavy
  cream
1 package (6 ounces) semisweet chocolate pieces

2 eggs
¼ cup sugar
1 teaspoon peppermint
  extract
6 ice cubes (about 1 cup)

In a 5-cup blender container, sprinkle unflavored gelatine over cold milk. Let stand 3 to 4 minutes. Add hot milk and process at low speed 2 minutes. Add cream, chocolate pieces, eggs, sugar, and peppermint extract; process at high speed until well blended, about 2 minutes. Add ice cubes, one at a time, and process at high speed until ice is melted. Pour immediately into dessert dishes. Chill until set.

BANANA NUT PARFAITS

6 servings

2 envelopes Knox
  Unflavored Gelatine
2 cups cold milk, divided
3 medium bananas, cut into
  chunks
2 tablespoons sugar
1 teaspoon vanilla extract

¼ teaspoon ground
  cinnamon
2 cups (1 pint) vanilla ice
  cream, solidly frozen
1 cup coarsely chopped
  walnuts

In a 5-cup blender container, sprinkle unflavored gelatine over ½ cup cold milk; let stand 3 to 4 minutes. Heat 1 cup milk to boiling; pour into blender. Cover and process at low speed 2 minutes. Add remaining ½ cup cold milk, bananas, sugar, vanilla, cinnamon, and ice cream; process at high speed until thoroughly blended. Let stand 7 minutes, or until mixture is slightly thick.

In parfait glasses or dessert dishes, alternately layer walnuts and banana mixture. Chill until set, 30 minutes to 1 hour.

FRUIT SALAD/DESSERT

6 servings

If you have something else planned to finish the meal, call this salad and everyone will be pleased—but you can also call this dessert and find that nobody will object at all

2 **envelopes Knox Unflavored Gelatine**	1 **can (1 pound) fruit cocktail**
½ **cup cold water**	
¾ **cup boiling water**	
1 **can (6 ounces) frozen lemonade concentrate, unthawed**	

In a medium bowl, mix unflavored gelatine with cold water. Add boiling water and stir until gelatine is completely dissolved. Stir in frozen concentrate until melted. Stir in fruit with its syrup. Chill, stirring occasionally, until mixture mounds slightly when dropped from a spoon. Mix well. Turn into a 4-cup mold; chill until firm. Unmold to serve.

76

FRESH FIVE-FRUIT SHIMMER

8 servings

3 **envelopes Knox Unflavored Gelatine**	½ **cup fresh lemon juice**
⅔ **cup sugar**	1 **cup fresh melon balls**
2 **cups boiling water**	1 **cup blueberries**
1 **cup cold water**	1 **cup sliced peaches**
	1 **cup pitted sweet cherries**

In a medium bowl, mix unflavored gelatine with sugar. Add boiling water and stir until gelatine is completely dissolved. Stir in cold water and lemon juice. Chill, stirring occasionally, until mixture is the consistency of unbeaten egg whites.

Fold in fruit. Turn into a 6-cup mold; chill until firm. Unmold to serve. If desired, garnish with whipped cream or with half-and-half mayonnaise and dairy sour cream.

Great go-alongs: *Let this ambrosial dish serve as both salad and dessert for a simple summer supper, with cold sliced roast beef or chicken and hot buttered rolls. Milk for the youngsters, iced tea for the adults.*

GINGER/MANDARIN DELIGHT

4 to 6 servings

Oranges for flavor, ginger ale for sparkle, make this quick-to-fix dessert an always-welcome family treat

2 cans (11 ounces each)
  mandarin oranges
2 envelopes Knox
  Unflavored Gelatine

¾ cup orange juice, heated
  to boiling
¼ cup lemon juice
½ cup ginger ale

Drain oranges, reserving syrup. In a 5-cup blender container, sprinkle unflavored gelatine over reserved syrup; let stand 3 to 4 minutes. Add boiling orange juice; process at low speed 2 minutes. Add oranges and lemon juice; process at high speed until oranges are puréed, about 2 minutes. Slowly add ginger ale; mix gently with spatula. Pour into a 4-cup mold or bowl; chill until firm. Unmold to serve.

FRUITED CALIFORNIA CREAM 8 servings

Delightful weight-conscious sweet at only 90 calories a serving —omit the honey and reduce to only 80

1 envelope Knox
  Unflavored Gelatine
1 cup cold buttermilk
1 cup orange juice, heated
  to boiling
2 tablespoons honey

1 medium banana, peeled
  and thinly sliced
1 orange, peeled and
  chunked
¼ cup seedless raisins

In a 5-cup blender container, sprinkle unflavored gelatine over buttermilk; let stand 3 to 4 minutes. Add hot orange juice and honey; process at low speed 2 minutes. Pour into a medium bowl. Chill, stirring occasionally, until mixture is the consistency of unbeaten egg whites.

Fold in remaining ingredients. Turn into 8 dessert dishes or a 4-cup bowl; chill until set, about 3 hours.

Another way: *If you don't like the tang of buttermilk, give this a milder flavor by substituting skim milk.*

TWENTY-MINUTE LEMON MOUSSE

8 servings

When you say to yourself, "Oops, I forgot to make dessert!" this rich-tasting, creamy mousse will come to your rescue

2 envelopes Knox
   Unflavored Gelatine
½ cup cold water
1 cup boiling water
2 cups (1 pint) lemon
   sherbet

1 container (9 ounces)
   frozen whipped
   topping, thawed

In a large bowl, mix unflavored gelatine with cold water. Add boiling water and stir until gelatine is completely dissolved. Gradually add sherbet; stir until completely melted. Blend in whipped topping. Spoon into dessert dishes; chill 15 minutes.

Other ways: *Use any flavor sherbet in this with excellent results—orange, pineapple, lime, raspberry, or any kind you have handy in the freezer.*

79

FRESH LEMON SNOW

6 to 8 servings

1 envelope Knox
   Unflavored Gelatine
¾ cup sugar
1¼ cups boiling water

1 teaspoon grated lemon
   peel
¼ cup lemon juice
2 egg whites

In a medium bowl, mix unflavored gelatine with sugar. Add boiling water and stir until gelatine is completely dissolved. Stir in lemon peel and juice. Chill, stirring occasionally, until mixture is slightly lumpy.

Turn into the large bowl of an electric mixer; add unbeaten egg whites. Beat at high speed until mixture is light and fluffy and begins to hold its shape, 7 to 10 minutes. Turn into a 5-cup serving bowl or individual serving dishes; chill until set.

Idea: *Make this delicious old-fashioned favorite even better by serving with fresh or frozen strawberries or raspberries.*

SUNNY CITRUS MEDLEY

8 servings

When you're deep in winter's doldrums, this delightful dessert can make you believe that spring is on its way

2 envelopes Knox
  Unflavored Gelatine
⅓ cup sugar
1 cup boiling water
1½ cups orange juice
1 cup ginger ale
½ teaspoon grated
  orange peel

1 package (3 ounces) cream
  cheese, softened
2 oranges, peeled and
  cut into chunks,
  divided
1 grapefruit, peeled and
  cut into chunks,
  divided

In a medium bowl, mix unflavored gelatine with sugar. Add boiling water and stir until gelatine is completely dissolved. Add orange juice, ginger ale, and orange peel.

In a small bowl, beat cream cheese until smooth; gradually beat in 1¼ cups gelatine mixture. Chill, stirring occasionally, until mixture is the consistency of unbeaten egg whites. Fold in a third of the fruit. Turn into a 5-cup mold; chill until almost set.

Meanwhile, chill remaining gelatine mixture, stirring occasionally, until mixture is the consistency of unbeaten egg whites. Fold in remaining fruit. Turn onto almost-set gelatine; chill until firm. Unmold to serve.

Company spectaculars

Something very special, something luscious and hand-some, something all your own, not made from a box or brought home and thawed—that's what you have in mind when you plan a dessert for company. Here are happy endings that meet all those requirements and more. Every one of these great desserts is your very own, flavored as you want it with your own choice of ingredi-ents. And every one can be prepared in advance, so there's no last-minute fuss after guests arrive.

IRISH MINT REFRESHER   about 8 servings

1 can (29 ounces) sliced
   pears
⅓ cup green crème de
   menthe
2 envelopes Knox
   Unflavored Gelatine

1 cup (8 ounces) dairy
   sour cream
⅓ cup sliced almonds

Drain pears, reserving syrup, and cut into bite-size pieces. In a medium bowl, marinate pears in crème de menthe.

In a medium saucepan, sprinkle unflavored gelatine over 1 cup reserved syrup. Let stand 1 minute. Stir over medium heat until gelatine is completely dissolved, about 1 minute. Remove from heat. To remaining syrup add enough water to make 1½ cups. Add to gelatine mixture with sour cream. Chill, stirring occasionally, until mixture is the consistency of unbeaten egg whites.

Fold in almonds and pears with crème de menthe. Turn into a 5-cup mold; chill until firm. Unmold to serve.

Great go-alongs: *Let this dessert provide the triumphant finale to a perfect dinner for guests. Start with Zesty Sea-food Appetizer (page 37), go on to veal scallops with lemon juice and capers, rice cooked in beef broth, orange and onion salad, and heated hard rolls. Serve white wine with the dinner, if you wish, and follow with a piping hot beverage.*

FRUIT 'N HONEY CELEBRATION

about 10 servings

Yogurt lovers know how good their favorite is mixed with fruit—here's a combination that will delight everyone, even those who say they can't stand yogurt!

1 can (11 ounces)
  mandarin oranges,
  in syrup
2 envelopes Knox
  Unflavored Gelatine
1½ cups orange juice,
  divided

1 tablespoon almond
  yogurt
2 tablespoons honey
½ cup raisins
½ cup chopped walnuts
2 bananas, cut into
  ½-inch slices

Drain oranges, reserving syrup. In a medium saucepan, mix unflavored gelatine with 1 cup orange juice. Let stand 1 minute. Stir over medium heat until gelatine is completely dissolved, about 1 minute. Remove from heat. With wire whip or rotary beater, blend in yogurt, remaining ½ cup orange juice, reserved syrup, and honey. Chill, stirring occasionally, until mixture is the consistency of unbeaten egg whites.

Fold in oranges, raisins, walnuts, and bananas. Turn into a 6-cup mold or individual dessert dishes; chill until firm. Unmold to serve.

Another way: *Substitute lemon yogurt for the vanilla yogurt, chopped pitted dates for the raisins.*

FLOATING ALMOND FRUIT FANTASY

8 servings

2 envelopes Knox
  Unflavored Gelatine,
  divided
10 tablespoons sugar,
  divided
1¾ cups boiling water,
  divided
1 can (5⅓ ounces)
  evaporated milk

1 tablespoon almond
  extract
1 can (11 ounces) mandarin
  oranges
Orange juice
1 cup sliced strawberries
1 cup blueberries

Reserve 1½ teaspoons unflavored gelatine.

In a medium bowl, mix remaining unflavored gelatine with 8 tablespoons sugar. Add 1¼ cups boiling water and stir until gelatine is completely dissolved. Stir in milk and almond extract. Turn into a 9-inch-square baking pan; chill until firm, about 2 hours.

Then, in a medium bowl, combine reserved gelatine with remaining 2 tablespoons sugar. Add remaining ½ cup boiling water and stir until gelatine is completely dissolved. Drain oranges, reserving syrup. Add enough orange juice to the syrup to make 1½ cups; add to gelatine mixture. Chill until mixture is slightly syrupy.

To serve, cut almond gelatine into 1-inch diamond shapes. In 8 individual dessert dishes, equally divide gelatine diamonds, mandarin oranges, strawberries, and blueberries; top with orange syrup.

ALMOND BRITTLE BAVARIAN

about 6 servings

½ cup sugar
¼ cup chopped blanched
   almonds
 1 envelope Knox
   Unflavored Gelatine
¼ cup cold water

¾ cup boiling water
 1 cup (½ pint) vanilla ice
   cream, softened
 1 cup (½ pint) heavy
   cream, whipped

In a small saucepan, melt sugar over medium heat, stirring constantly until syrupy and light brown in color; stir in almonds. Pour onto greased baking sheet; cool. Between wax paper, crush brittle fine; reserve 2 tablespoons.

In a small bowl, mix unflavored gelatine with cold water. Add boiling water and stir until gelatine is completely dissolved. Add ice cream; stir until melted. Let stand until mixture mounds slightly when dropped from a spoon, about 7 minutes; fold in whipped cream and brittle. Turn into dessert dishes or a 1-quart bowl; chill until set. Garnish with reserved brittle.

Another way: *Substitute chopped pecans for the almonds to make Praline Brittle Bavarian.*

SABAYON SNOW

Luscious, airy dessert to serve weight-conscious guests—each serving has only 40 calories without sauce; 35 calories for each tablespoon of sauce

1 envelope Knox Unflavored Gelatine	⅓ cup Marsala
1¼ cups cold water, divided	2 egg whites
3 tablespoons sugar	Custard Sauce (recipe follows)

In a medium saucepan, mix unflavored gelatine with ½ cup cold water. Let stand 1 minute. Stir over medium heat until gelatine is completely dissolved, about 1 minute. Remove from heat. Stir in sugar and remaining ¾ cup cold water. Stir in Marsala. Chill, stirring occasionally, until mixture mounds slightly when dropped from a spoon.

84

Place in the large bowl of an electric mixer with 2 unbeaten egg whites. Beat at high speed about 10 minutes, until mixture becomes light and tripled in volume. Turn into a 5-cup bowl or individual dishes; chill until set. If desired, garnish with twisted lemon slice and mint sprigs. Serve with Custard Sauce.

CUSTARD SAUCE

about 2 cups

¼ cup sugar	1½ cups skimmed milk
1 teaspoon cornstarch	3 egg yolks
1 teaspoon grated lemon peel	1 teaspoon vanilla extract

In the top of a double boiler, combine sugar, cornstarch, and lemon peel. Gradually stir in milk. Place over boiling water and cook, stirring frequently, until mixture thickens slightly.

In a small bowl, beat egg yolks. Stir a little of the hot mixture into the yolks, then stir all back into the double boiler. Cook, stirring constantly, until mixture is thick enough to coat a spoon. Remove from heat; stir in vanilla. Chill.

RASPBERRIES 'N CREAM FANCY

10 servings

2 envelopes Knox
   Unflavored Gelatine
⅔ cup sugar, divided
3 eggs, separated
1 cup milk

2 cups (16 ounces) red
   raspberry yogurt
Red food coloring (optional)
1 cup (½ pint) heavy
   cream, whipped

In a medium saucepan, mix unflavored gelatine with ⅓ cup sugar. Beat egg yolks with milk; blend into gelatine mixture. Stir over low heat until gelatine is completely dissolved, 5 to 8 minutes. Remove from heat. With a wire whip or rotary beater, blend in yogurt and food coloring. Chill, stirring occasionally, until mixture mounds slightly when dropped from a spoon.

In a medium bowl, beat egg whites until soft peaks form; gradually add remaining ⅓ cup sugar and beat until stiff. Fold in gelatine mixture and whipped cream. Turn into individual dessert dishes or an 8-cup bowl; chill until set.

85

SHIMMERY SANGRIA

12 servings

3 envelopes Knox
   Unflavored Gelatine
1 cup fresh orange juice
½ cup sugar
¼ cup fresh lemon juice
2½ cups red wine
1 bottle (7 ounces) club
   soda

2 oranges, peeled and
   sliced crosswise
1 banana, peeled and cut
   into 1-inch slices
2 peaches, peeled and
   sliced
1 cup halved strawberries

In a medium saucepan, mix gelatine with cold orange juice. Let stand 1 minute. Stir over medium heat until gelatine is completely dissolved, about 1 minute. Remove from heat. Add sugar; stir until dissolved. Add lemon juice, wine, and club soda. Chill, stirring occasionally, until mixture is the consistency of unbeaten egg whites.

Fold in fruit. Turn into an 8-cup mold; chill until firm, several hours or overnight. Unmold and, if desired, garnish with additional fresh fruit.

BLACK FOREST SOUFFLE about 8 servings

1 can (16 ounces) sour
  pitted cherries, drained
5 tablespoons kirsch,
  divided
4 squares (1 ounce each)
  semisweet chocolate,
  divided
2 envelopes Knox
  Unflavored Gelatine

¾ cup sugar, divided
3 eggs, separated
2 cups milk
1½ teaspoons vanilla
  extract
2 cups (1 pint) heavy
  cream, divided

Chop cherries and marinate in 2 tablespoons kirsch.

Using about ¼ ounce chocolate, make enough choco-late curls for garnish.

In a medium saucepan, mix unflavored gelatine with ½ cup sugar. Beat egg yolks with milk and add to gelatine mixture with remaining chocolate squares (about 3¾ ounces). Stir over low heat until gelatine is completely dissolved and chocolate melts, 5 to 8 minutes. Remove from heat. Add remaining 3 tablespoons kirsch and vanilla. With wire whip or rotary beater, beat mixture until chocolate is well blended. Chill, stirring occasion-ally, until mixture mounds slightly when dropped from a spoon.

In a large bowl, beat egg whites until soft peaks form; gradually add remaining ¼ cup sugar and beat until stiff. Fold in gelatine mixture.

In a medium bowl, whip 1¾ cups heavy cream and fold into gelatine mixture with chopped cherries and kirsch. Turn into a 1-quart soufflé dish with a 3-inch collar (see below). Chill until set, about 4 hours. Remove collar. To garnish, top with remaining heavy cream, whipped, and chocolate curls.

Idea: *To make a collar for a soufflé dish, tear off a piece of wax paper or foil 4 inches longer than the circumference of the dish. Fold it in thirds lengthwise. Place it around the top of the dish and tape, clip, or staple it together so that it fits snugly.*

SPIRITED CHOCOLATE SOUFFLE

16 servings

2 envelopes Knox
    Unflavored Gelatine
½ cup cold water
⅔ cup crème de cacao
1 package (12 ounces)
    semisweet chocolate
    pieces

8 eggs, separated
⅓ cup firmly packed light
    brown sugar
2 cups (1 pint) heavy
    cream, whipped

In a medium saucepan, mix gelatine with water and crème de cacao. Let stand 1 minute. Stir over low heat until gelatine is completely dissolved, about 5 minutes. Add chocolate pieces; stir until melted. Remove from heat; beat in egg yolks one at a time. Cool.

In a large bowl, beat egg whites until soft peaks form; gradually add brown sugar and beat until stiff. Fold in chocolate mixture and whipped cream. Turn into a 2-quart soufflé dish with a 2-inch collar (page 87). Chill until set, several hours or overnight. Remove collar to serve. Garnish with whipped cream, if desired.

STRAWBERRIES 'N CREAM SOUFFLE

about 12 servings

6 cups sliced fresh
    strawberries (about
    3 pints), divided
2 envelopes Knox
    Unflavored Gelatine
¾ cup sugar, divided

4 eggs, separated
1 cup milk
⅓ cup brandy
1 cup (½ pint) heavy
    cream, whipped

In 5-cup blender container, purée 3 cups strawberries.

In a medium saucepan, mix unflavored gelatine with ½ cup sugar. Beat egg yolks with milk and blend into gelatine mixture. Stir over low heat until gelatine is completely dissolved, 5 to 8 minutes. Turn gelatine mixture into a large bowl; stir in puréed strawberries and brandy. Chill, stirring occasionally, until mixture mounds slightly when dropped from a spoon.

In a medium bowl, beat egg whites until soft peaks form; gradually add remaining ¼ cup sugar and beat until stiff. Fold in gelatine mixture, whipped cream, and remaining strawberry slices. Turn into a 1½-quart soufflé dish with a 3-inch collar (page 87). Chill until firm, about 4 hours. Remove collar to serve.

LEMON-BERRY SOUFFLE   6 to 8 servings

2 envelopes Knox
  Unflavored Gelatine
	1 tablespoon grated lemon
	  peel

½ cup sugar, divided	1 cup (½ pint) heavy
4 eggs, separated	cream, whipped
2¼ cups water	1 pint blueberries (about
½ cup lemon juice	2 cups)

In a medium saucepan, mix unflavored gelatine with ¼ cup sugar. Beat egg yolks with water and blend into gelatine mixture. Stir over low heat until gelatine is completely dissolved, about 5 minutes. Remove from heat; stir in lemon juice and peel. Chill, stirring occasionally, until mixture mounds slightly when dropped from a spoon.

89

In a large bowl, beat egg whites until soft peaks form; gradually add remaining ¼ cup sugar and beat until stiff. Fold in gelatine mixture, whipped cream, and blueberries. Turn into a 1½-quart soufflé dish with a 2-inch collar (page 87). Chill until firm, about 4 hours. Remove collar to serve.

MINTED GELATI   about 1 quart

1 envelope Knox Unflavored Gelatine	2 cups whole milk
¼ cup sugar	¼ cup crème de menthe
1 cup nonfat dry milk powder	

In a medium saucepan, combine gelatine, sugar, and nonfat dry milk. Add milk. Stir over low heat until gelatine is completely dissolved, about 5 minutes. Remove from heat and cool; stir in crème de menthe. Pour mixture into two 9- x 9- x 2-inch pans. Freeze until firm around edges, about 1½ hours.

Spoon into a large bowl; beat until smooth. Return to pans and freeze until firm, 3 to 4 hours.

LIGHT AND LUSCIOUS PIE   8 servings

A lovely, fruity dessert with three equally delicious variations, any of which you'll serve guests proudly—if there's to be a crowd, make two pies, three, four!

1 envelope Knox
   Unflavored Gelatine
⅔ cup sugar, divided
2 eggs, separated
⅔ cup milk
1 cup (8 ounces) apricot
   yogurt

1 to 2 tablespoons apricot-
   flavored brandy
   (optional)
Chocolate Crumb Crust
   (recipe follows)

In a medium saucepan, mix unflavored gelatine with ⅓ cup sugar. Beat egg yolks with milk and blend into gelatine mixture. Stir over low heat until gelatine is completely dissolved, 5 to 8 minutes. Remove from heat. With wire whip or rotary beater, blend in yogurt and brandy. Chill, stirring occasionally, until mixture mounds slightly when dropped from a spoon.

In a medium bowl, beat egg whites until soft peaks form; gradually add remaining ⅓ cup sugar and beat until stiff. Fold in gelatine mixture. Turn into prepared Chocolate Crumb Crust and chill until firm, about 3 hours. Garnish with additional chocolate wafer crumbs, if desired.

CHOCOLATE CRUMB CRUST

1¼ cups chocolate wafer
   crumbs

¼ cup melted butter or
   margarine

In a small bowl, combine crumbs and butter. Press into a 9-inch pie plate. Chill.

Other ways: *Try peach yogurt with peach-flavored brandy, coffee yogurt with coffee liqueur, or cherry yogurt with cherry liqueur.*

THINK-SPRING CHIFFON PIE   8 servings

1 envelope Knox
   Unflavored Gelatine
½ cup sugar, divided
2 eggs, separated
1 cup milk

¼ cup cream sherry
1 cup (½ pint) heavy
   cream, whipped
Macaroon Crumb Crust
   (recipe follows)

In a medium saucepan, mix unflavored gelatine with ¼ cup sugar. Beat egg yolks with milk and blend into gelatine mixture. Stir over low heat until gelatine is completely dissolved, 5 to 8 minutes. Remove from heat; stir in sherry. Chill, stirring occasionally, until mixture mounds slightly when dropped from a spoon.

In a medium bowl, beat egg whites until soft peaks form; gradually add remaining ¼ cup sugar and beat until stiff. Fold in gelatine mixture and whipped cream. Turn into prepared Macaroon Crumb Crust and chill until firm, about 3 hours. Garnish with additional whipped cream and toasted coconut, if desired.

MACAROON CRUMB CRUST

1½ cups crisp macaroon
   cookie crumbs

¼ cup butter or margarine,
   softened

Preheat oven to 375° F. In a small bowl, combine crumbs and butter; press into a 9-inch pie plate. Bake 8 minutes; cool, then chill.

Great go-alongs: *This pie is the perfect climax to a think-spring company meal—serve broiled chicken, asparagus with lemon butter, heated rye rolls, watercress and tomato salad with Wish-Bone Chunky Blue Cheese Dressing.*

CREAMY CHOCOLATE-PECAN PIE 8 servings

1 envelope Knox Unflavored Gelatine	1 teaspoon vanilla extract
⅓ cup dark brown sugar	1 tablespoon granulated sugar
2 eggs, separated	1 cup (½ pint) heavy cream, whipped
1 cup milk	
½ cup semisweet chocolate pieces	1 cup coarsely chopped pecans
⅓ cup dark corn syrup	Vanilla Crumb Crust (recipe follows)
2 tablespoons butter or margarine	

In a medium saucepan, mix unflavored gelatine with brown sugar. Beat egg yolks with milk and blend into gelatine mixture. Stir over low heat until gelatine is completely dissolved, 5 to 8 minutes. Add chocolate pieces, corn syrup, butter, and vanilla; stir over low heat until chocolate is completely melted, about 5 minutes. Chill, stirring occasionally, until mixture mounds slightly when dropped from a spoon.

92

In a large bowl, beat egg whites until soft peaks form; gradually add sugar and beat until stiff. Fold in gelatine mixture, whipped cream, and pecans. Turn into prepared Vanilla Crumb Crust and chill until firm, about 3 hours.

VANILLA CRUMB CRUST

1¼ cups vanilla wafer crumbs (about 30 1¾-inch wafers)	2 tablespoons melted butter or margarine

In a small bowl, combine crumbs and butter. Press into a 9-inch pie plate. Chill.

EASY BRANDY ALEXANDER PIE 8 servings

2 envelopes Knox Unflavored Gelatine	3 tablespoons crème de cacao
1½ cups (¾ pint) half 'n' half or light cream, divided	1 cup ice cubes (6 to 8)
¼ cup sugar	Chocolate-Coconut Crust (recipe follows) or 9-inch graham cracker crust*
3 tablespoons brandy	

In a 5-cup blender container, sprinkle unflavored gelatine over ¾ cup cold half 'n' half. Let stand 3 to 4 minutes. Heat remaining ¾ cup half 'n' half to boiling. Pour into blender; process at low speed 2 minutes. Add sugar, brandy, crème de cacao; add ice cubes, one at a time, and process at high speed until ice is melted. Pour into prepared Chocolate-Coconut Crust and chill until firm, about 30 minutes.

CHOCOLATE-COCONUT CRUST

1 envelope (1 ounce) unsweetened chocolate, premelted	2 tablespoons milk
	2 cups flaked coconut
	½ cup confectioners sugar

In a medium bowl, combine chocolate and milk. Stir in remaining ingredients. Press into a 9-inch pie plate.

*See recipe on page 109; use half of each ingredient for one 9-inch crust.

APRICOT TRIFLE PIE   8 servings

1 envelope Knox Unflavored Gelatine	12 ladyfingers
½ cup sugar, divided	½ cup apricot jam
2 eggs, separated	1 cup (½ pint) heavy cream, whipped
1 cup milk	8 canned apricot halves, well drained and chilled
¼ cup cream sherry	

In a medium saucepan, mix unflavored gelatine with ¼ cup sugar. Beat egg yolks and milk together, stir into gelatine mixture. Stir over low heat until gelatine is completely dissolved and mixture thickens slightly, 6 to 8 minutes. Remove from heat; stir in sherry. Chill, stirring occasionally, until mixture mounds slightly when dropped from a spoon.

Meanwhile, split ladyfingers; cut pieces to stand, crust side out, around sides of a 9-inch pie plate. Arrange remaining ladyfingers and pieces, crust side down, on bottom of pan. Heat apricot jam; strain and brush over surface of ladyfingers. Reserve remaining jam. When gelatine mixture is chilled, beat egg whites until soft peaks form; gradually add remaining ¼ cup sugar and beat until stiff. Fold in gelatine mixture and whipped cream. Turn into prepared pie plate; chill until set. Glaze apricot halves with reserved jam. Garnish top of pie with apricot halves.

Chilly cheesecakes

Cheesecakes are superb, but they're a lot of trouble? Not necessarily. Made the unflavored gelatine way, cheesecakes are a breeze—a beautiful, scrumptious breeze! Tangy with lemon, spectacular with fresh fruit, rich with chocolate or butterscotch, here are traditional-style cheesecakes and great cheesecake pies, all your own make-ahead triumphs.

BUTTERSCOTCH SWIRL CHEESECAKE
10 to 12 servings

Graham Cracker-Walnut
    Crust (page 96)
2 envelopes Knox
    Unflavored Gelatine
2⅓ cups milk, divided
4 eggs, separated
1 teaspoon vanilla extract

2 packages (8 ounces
    each) cream cheese,
    softened
1 package (6 ounces)
    butterscotch-flavored
    pieces
¼ cup sugar

Prepare Graham Cracker-Walnut Crust; chill.

In a medium saucepan, mix unflavored gelatine with 1 cup milk. Beat egg yolks with 1 cup milk and stir into gelatine mixture. Stir over low heat until gelatine is completely dissolved, about 5 minutes. Remove from heat; add vanilla.

In a large bowl, beat cream cheese until smooth; gradually beat in gelatine mixture. Chill, stirring occasionally, until mixture mounds slightly when dropped from a spoon.

In a small saucepan, melt butterscotch pieces with remaining ⅓ cup milk; cool.

In a medium bowl, beat egg whites until soft peaks form; gradually add sugar and beat until stiff. Fold in gelatine mixture.

Combine butterscotch with 2 cups gelatine mixture and alternate spoonfuls with remaining gelatine mixture in prepared crust. Gently swirl with a knife to marble. Chill until firm, about 4 hours.

GRAHAM CRACKER-WALNUT CRUST

1 cup graham cracker
    crumbs
3 tablespoons melted butter
    or margarine

½ cup finely chopped
    walnuts

In a small bowl, combine all ingredients. Press onto bottom of a 9-inch springform pan.

IT'S-A-SNAP CHEESECAKE about 8 servings

1 envelope Knox
    Unflavored Gelatine
½ cup sugar
1 cup boiling water
2 packages (8 ounces
    each) cream cheese,
    softened

1 teaspoon vanilla extract
    (optional)
9-inch graham cracker
    crust*

In a large bowl, mix unflavored gelatine with sugar. Add boiling water and stir until gelatine is dissolved. With electric mixer, beat in cream cheese and vanilla until smooth. Pour into prepared crust; chill until firm, about 2 hours. Top, if desired, with fresh or canned fruit.

*See recipe on page 109; use half of each ingredient for one 9-inch crust. Or, to save time, buy a prepared crust.

PINEAPPLE CHEESECAKE 10 servings

Full of tart-sweet goodness and only 90 calories a serving

1 can (20 ounces) pineapple
    chunks in natural juice
1 envelope Knox
    Unflavored Gelatine
½ cup skim milk

1 package (8 ounces)
    imitation cream cheese,
    softened
1 teaspoon vanilla extract
2 egg whites

Drain pineapple, reserving liquid. Chop enough pineapple to make ¾ cup; reserve.

In a medium saucepan, mix unflavored gelatine with milk; let stand 1 minute. Stir over low heat until gelatine is dissolved, about 3 minutes. Remove from heat.

In a large bowl, beat cream cheese until smooth; gradually beat in hot gelatine mixture and vanilla. To reserved pineapple juice add enough water to make 1 cup; gradually beat into cream cheese mixture. Chill, stirring occasionally, until mixture mounds slightly when dropped from a spoon.

In a medium bowl, beat egg whites until stiff, but not dry. Fold in gelatine mixture and chopped pineapple. Turn into a 9-inch pie plate and chill until firm, about 4 hours. Garnish with remaining pineapple.

LUSCIOUS LEMON CHEESECAKE

12 servings

Creamy no-bake cheesecake with only 150 calories a serving

2 envelopes Knox
 Unflavored Gelatine
¾ cup sugar, divided
2 eggs, separated
1½ cups skim milk, divided
1½ tablespoons lemon juice
1½ teaspoons grated lemon
 peel
3 cups (24 ounces) lowfat
 creamed cottage
 cheese

⅓ cup graham cracker
 crumbs (about five 2½-
 inch-square crackers)
¼ teaspoon ground
 cinnamon
⅛ teaspoon ground nutmeg

In a medium saucepan, mix unflavored gelatine with ½ cup sugar. Beat egg yolks with milk and blend into gelatine mixture. Stir over low heat until gelatine is completely dissolved, about 5 minutes. Remove from heat; add remaining ½ cup milk and lemon juice and peel.

In a large bowl, beat cottage cheese until smooth; gradually beat in gelatine mixture. Chill, stirring occasionally, until mixture mounds slightly when dropped from a spoon.

In a large bowl, beat egg whites until soft peaks form; gradually add remaining ¼ cup sugar and beat until stiff. Fold in cheese mixture. Turn into an 8- or 9-inch springform pan. Combine graham cracker crumbs, cinnamon, and nutmeg and sprinkle over top. Chill until firm, about 3 hours.

Another way: *Mix gelatine with artificial sweetener equal to ½ cup sugar; cuts calories to 110 per serving.*

ITALIAN CHEESECAKE

12 to 16 servings

Viva Italia! This memorable dessert looks and tastes as if you'd labored all day to achieve it, but it's make-ahead easy—the crowning touch for a satisfying company meal

CRUST

1 cup brown-edge wafer
   cookie crumbs

¼ cup butter or margarine,
   melted

FILLING

2 envelopes Knox
   Unflavored Gelatine

¾ cup sugar, divided

4 eggs, separated

1 cup milk

4 cups (2 pounds) ricotta
   cheese

⅓ cup finely chopped
   semisweet chocolate
   pieces

¼ cup finely chopped
   mixed candied fruit

¼ cup finely chopped
   blanched almonds

¼ cup orange liqueur

1 teaspoon grated lemon
   peel

1 teaspoon vanilla extract

Combine cookie crumbs and melted butter; press onto the bottom of a 9-inch springform pan. Refrigerate. In a medium saucepan, mix unflavored gelatine with ¼ cup sugar. Beat egg yolks with milk; stir into gelatine mixture. Stir over low heat until gelatine is completely dissolved, about 5 minutes. Remove from heat.

In a medium bowl, beat ricotta until smooth and creamy; add to gelatine mixture with remaining ingredients. Mix well.

Beat egg whites until soft peaks form; gradually add remaining ½ cup sugar and beat until stiff. Fold in gelatine mixture. Turn into prepared springform pan; chill until firm, about 5 hours. To serve, loosen around edge of pan with a sharp knife; release spring and remove sides of pan. Place on a serving plate, and garnish with small clusters of grapes, if desired.

Great go-alongs: *For an Italian dinner with no pasta, here's a lighter meal that will blend easily with this great dessert. Serve a huge tossed green salad with oil and vinegar dressing. Accompany it with a platter of antipasto-type goodies: sliced tomatoes sprinkled with basil, pimien-*

tos crisscrossed with anchovies, sliced salami, wedges of melon draped with prosciutto, halved hard-cooked eggs, sliced red onions, pickled baby eggplants (from a jar), thin strips of provolone. With this, lots of crusty garlic bread and a sturdy red wine.

GERMAN CHOCOLATE CHEESECAKE

about 9 servings

One of the great all-time favorite desserts is German Chocolate Cake—here is a wonderful cheesecake version that has lost none of its sweet appeal in the translation

- **1 bar (4 ounces) sweet cooking chocolate**
- **2 cups milk, divided**
- **¼ cup butter or margarine**
- **1 cup flaked coconut**
- **1 cup finely chopped pecans**
- **2 envelopes Knox Unflavored Gelatine**
- **¾ cup sugar, divided**
- **3 eggs, separated**
- **2 teaspoons vanilla extract**
- **2 packages (8 ounces each) cream cheese, softened**

99

In a small saucepan, over low heat, melt chocolate with ¼ cup milk; reserve ⅓ cup of mixture. To remaining chocolate mixture, add butter, stirring until it melts. Stir in coconut and pecans. Press mixture onto bottom of a 9-inch-square baking pan and chill.

In a medium saucepan, mix unflavored gelatine with ½ cup sugar. Beat egg yolks with remaining 1¾ cups milk; blend into gelatine mixture. Stir over low heat until gelatine is completely dissolved, about 5 minutes. Remove from heat; add vanilla.

In a large bowl, beat cream cheese until smooth; gradually beat in gelatine mixture. Chill, stirring occasionally, until mixture mounds slightly when dropped from a spoon.

In a small bowl, beat egg whites until soft peaks form; gradually add remaining ¼ cup sugar and beat until stiff. Fold in cheese mixture. Into 2 cups cheese mixture, blend reserved chocolate; alternate spoonfuls of chocolate and plain mixtures in prepared pan. Gently swirl with a knife to marble; chill until firm. To serve, cut into squares. Garnish with pecan halves, if desired.

Especially for the kids

Children's love of sweets is notorious—to most of them, a meal without dessert is a waste of time. Here you can learn—with Knox Unflavored Gelatine to show you how —lots of new ways with old-favorite flavors that are perennial kid-pleasers. And you can be sure that there's not one of these treats that the whole family won't love.

MARSHMALLOWS

about 100 squares

2 envelopes Knox
    Unflavored Gelatine
½ cup cold water
½ cup sugar

1 cup light corn syrup
1½ teaspoons vanilla
    extract
Confectioners sugar

In a medium saucepan, mix unflavored gelatine with cold water. Let stand 1 minute. Stir over medium heat until gelatine is completely dissolved, about 1 minute. Add sugar, corn syrup, and vanilla.

In a large bowl, beat gelatine mixture at high speed of electric mixer until mixture thickens and is a soft marshmallow consistency, about 15 minutes.

Line a 13- x 9- x 2-inch baking pan with wax paper; grease paper lightly. Spread mixture evenly in pan. Let stand at room temperature 4 hours or overnight.

Dust cutting board heavily with confectioners sugar. Turn out marshmallow mixture and carefully peel off wax paper. Cut into 1-inch squares and roll in additional confectioners sugar.

Other ways: *For Coconut Marshmallows, stir in ½ cup flaked coconut. For Chocolate Marshmallows, reduce corn syrup to ¾ cup; add ¼ cup chocolate-flavored syrup. For Mint Marshmallows, reduce vanilla extract to 1 teaspoon; add ¼ teaspoon mint extract and 4 drops green or red food coloring (optional). For Mint Chip Marshmallows, follow directions for Mint Marshmallows and stir in ½ cup small semisweet chocolate pieces.*

PEANUT BUTTER 'N JELLY BLOX

60 to 80 squares

As an after-lunch sweet, dinner dessert, anytime snack, even as breakfast to tempt a finicky appetite, these great flavor treats are just right for the show-and-tell set

4 envelopes Knox
    Unflavored Gelatine
	1 glass (10 ounces) grape
	    or other jelly

2 cups water, divided	½ cup peanut butter

In a large bowl, mix unflavored gelatine with ½ cup cold water. In a saucepan, combine jelly and remaining 1½ cups water; stir over medium heat until water boils and jelly is melted. Add to gelatine mixture and stir until gelatine is completely dissolved. Add peanut butter; beat with wire whip or rotary beater until well blended. Pour into an 8- or 9-inch-square pan; chill until firm. To serve, cut into 1-inch squares.

CHOCOLATE FRUIT-NUT BLOX

60 to 80 squares

Chocolate rates high as many youngsters' favorite flavor, and raisins and nuts aren't far down on the list—combine them, and you have a wholesome, better-than-a-candy-bar snack

4 envelopes Knox Unflavored Gelatine	½ cup raisins ½ cup chopped walnuts
½ cup sugar	
1 cup boiling water	

1 can (16 ounces)
    chocolate-flavored
    syrup	

In a medium bowl, mix unflavored gelatine with sugar. Add boiling water and stir until gelatine is completely dissolved. Blend in remaining ingredients. Pour into an 8- or 9-inch-square pan; chill until firm. To serve, cut into 1-inch squares.

Other ways: *Omit raisins; substitute tiny snipped bits of dried apricots, figs, or prunes. Substitute pecans or peanuts for the walnuts.*

CREME AND CRUNCHY PARFAITS

4 to 6 servings

1 envelope Knox
  Unflavored Gelatine
½ cup cold milk
½ cup milk, heated to
  boiling
1 cup marshmallow creme

½ teaspoon vanilla extract
1 cup ice cubes (6 to 8)
½ cup chocolate wafer
  crumbs
½ cup finely chopped
  walnuts

In a 5-cup blender container, sprinkle unflavored gelatine over cold milk; let stand 3 to 4 minutes. Add hot milk; process at low speed 2 minutes. Add marshmallow creme and vanilla. Add ice cubes, one at a time, and process at high speed until ice is melted. Let stand until mixture is thickened, about 7 minutes.

In a small bowl, combine chocolate crumbs and nuts.

In parfait glasses or dessert dishes, alternately layer marshmallow mixture with crumb-nut mixture. Chill until set, about 40 minutes.

103

PERKY PEPPERMINT PARFAITS

6 servings

2 envelopes Knox
  Unflavored Gelatine
½ cup cold milk
1 cup milk, heated to
  boiling
1 cup (½ pint) heavy
  cream
⅓ cup sugar

2 teaspoons vanilla
  extract
3 drops red food coloring
¼ cup peppermint candies
1 cup ice cubes (6 to 8)
1½ cups chocolate wafer
  crumbs

In a 5-cup blender container, sprinkle unflavored gelatine over cold milk; let stand 3 to 4 minutes. Add hot milk; process at low speed 2 minutes. Add heavy cream, sugar, vanilla, food coloring, and peppermint candies. Add ice cubes, one at a time, and process at high speed until ice is melted. Let stand until mixture is slightly thickened, about 10 minutes.

In parfait glasses or dessert dishes, alternately layer chocolate crumbs with peppermint mixture. Chill until set, about 40 minutes.

RASPBERRY RAGE

8 servings

Youngsters really go for their favorite fruit-punch drink turned into a pretty, tasty dessert—adults will enjoy it, too, if the kids leave any for them

2 packages (10 ounces each) frozen raspberries, thawed
2 envelopes Knox Unflavored Gelatine

2¼ cups red tropical fruit punch, divided
½ cup coarsely chopped pecans (optional)

Drain raspberries, reserving the syrup. In a medium saucepan, sprinkle unflavored gelatine over 1 cup fruit punch. Let stand 1 minute. Stir over medium heat until gelatine is completely dissolved, about 1 minute. Remove from heat. Add water to reserved syrup to equal 1½ cups; add to gelatine mixture with remaining 1¼ cups fruit punch. Chill, stirring occasionally, until mixture is the consistency of unbeaten egg whites. Into 3 cups gelatine mixture fold raspberries and pecans. Turn into a 5-cup mold; chill until almost set.

In a small bowl, beat remaining gelatine mixture until light and fluffy and doubled in volume. Pour over almost-set gelatine; chill until firm. Unmold to serve.

PEANUTTY POPS

6 servings

1 envelope Knox Unflavored Gelatine
½ cup sugar
1 cup boiling water

1 cup peanut butter (chunky or plain)
1 cup chocolate milk

In a medium bowl, mix unflavored gelatine with sugar. Add boiling water and stir until gelatine is completely dissolved. With wire whip or rotary beater, blend in peanut butter. Stir in chocolate milk. Pour into 5-ounce paper cups and place in freezer until partially frozen. Insert wooden ice cream sticks and freeze until firm.

Other ways: *Stir in small semisweet chocolate pieces, chopped banana, or mini-marshmallows just before inserting stick.*

CHOCOLATE-BANANA MILKSHAKE PUDDING

8 servings

Here's a great-tasting dessert that's also easy on the budget —children love it, and the grown-ups will make sure they also get their share

- 2 envelopes Knox Unflavored Gelatine
- ½ cup cold water
- 1 cup boiling water
- ¼ cup sugar
- 2 tablespoons unsweetened cocoa
- ⅔ cup nonfat dry milk powder
- 2 ripe bananas, peeled and chunked
- 1 teaspoon vanilla extract
- 2 cups ice cubes or crushed ice (12 to 16 cubes)

In a 5-cup blender container, sprinkle gelatine over cold water; let stand 3 to 4 minutes. Add boiling water; cover and process at low speed until gelatine is completely dissolved. Add sugar, cocoa, and dry milk; cover and process until smooth. Add bananas and vanilla. Add ice cubes, one at a time, and process at high speed until ice is melted.

105

Pour mixture into individual dessert dishes or custard cups. Chill until set, 20 to 30 minutes.

Idea: *Be sure to use ripe bananas for best flavor—sign of a ripe banana is little flecks of brown on the peel.*

Crowd-pleasers

When you're going to feed a lot of people, and you want to feed them well, you need help. That's when you'll be doubly grateful to Knox for these wonderful, flavorful desserts, great because they're made your way, with your own choice of ingredients. And you can prepare them hours before the crowd descends on you—even the day before, if you like. Prepare for compliments!

ENGLISH TRIFLE

16 servings

2 packages (10 ounces each) frozen raspberries, thawed
8- or 9-inch angel food or sponge cake, cut into 1-inch cubes (about 12 cups cubes)
1 cup cream sherry, divided
2 envelopes Knox Unflavored Gelatine

⅓ cup sugar
6 egg yolks
4 cups milk, divided
1 cup (½ pint) heavy cream, whipped
½ cup slivered almonds
1 tablespoon cornstarch

Drain raspberries, reserving syrup. In a large bowl, sprinkle cake cubes with mixture of ½ cup sherry and ½ cup reserved syrup; toss gently.

In a medium saucepan, mix unflavored gelatine with sugar. Beat egg yolks with 1 cup milk; blend into gelatine mixture. Stir over low heat until gelatine is completely dissolved and mixture thickens slightly, 5 to 8 minutes. Turn into a large bowl; add remaining 3 cups milk and ½ cup sherry. Chill, stirring occasionally, until mixture mounds slightly when dropped from a spoon. Fold in whipped cream, then raspberries.

In a 4-quart glass serving or punch bowl, layer trifle by arranging half the cake cubes, almonds, and gelatine mixture; repeat layering. Chill until set.

Meanwhile, in a small saucepan, mix cornstarch and remaining reserved syrup with enough water to equal 1 cup. Stir over medium heat until mixture thickens and clears; remove from heat and chill. If desired, garnish trifle with additional whipped cream and slivered almonds. Serve with raspberry sauce.

Great go-alongs: *Since this dessert, brought from the mother country, was a great favorite with our colonial ancestors, serve a complete New England dinner—the one, in fact, that was favored at Fourth of July celebrations in this country's earlier days. For the main course, poached salmon accompanied by creamed new potatoes and peas, Anadama Bread or Sally Lunn, mixed pickles. Cider to drink. Or make it a Deep South Colonial dinner of country-style ham, white cornmeal spoon bread, watermelon pickles, cole slaw with carrots and green peppers.*

CHOCOLATE MINI-MOUSSES

about 30 servings

2 envelopes Knox Unflavored Gelatine
½ cup sugar
3 cups milk
1 package (12 ounces) semisweet chocolate pieces

1 tablespoon vanilla extract
2 cups (1 pint) heavy cream, whipped

In a medium saucepan, mix unflavored gelatine with sugar; add milk and chocolate pieces. Stir over low heat until gelatine is completely dissolved and chocolate is melted, about 10 minutes. Turn into a large bowl; add vanilla. Beat with wire whip or rotary beater until chocolate is blended. Chill, stirring occasionally, until mixture mounds slightly when dropped from a spoon.

Fold in whipped cream. Set cupcake liners in muffin pan cups; spoon gelatine mixture into liners. Chill until set. Garnish with whipped cream, if desired.

Another way: *Pile this filling into 16 baked 3-inch tart shells or into two deep 9-inch baked pie shells. Whip 1 cup heavy cream with 1 teaspoon instant coffee powder, 2 tablespoons confectioners sugar, and ½ teaspoon cinnamon. Garnish tarts or pies with this mixture; sprinkle with grated semisweet chocolate.*

STRAWBERRY
CREAM 'N CUSTARD

12 servings

STRAWBERRY LAYER

2 envelopes Knox
  Unflavored Gelatine
½ cup cold milk
1 cup milk, heated to
  boiling
½ cup sugar
2 eggs

1 cup (½ pint) heavy
  cream
1 pint fresh strawberries
  (about 2 cups)
Several drops red food
  coloring
1 cup ice cubes (6 to 8)

In a 5-cup blender container, sprinkle unflavored gelatine over cold milk; let stand 3 to 4 minutes. Add hot milk; cover and process at low speed 2 minutes. Add sugar, eggs, heavy cream, strawberries, and food coloring. Add ice cubes, one at a time, and process at high speed until ice is melted.

Pour into a 2-quart clear-glass soufflé dish with a 3-inch collar (page 87) or into a 3-quart glass serving bowl. Chill until set, about 30 minutes.

CREAM 'N CUSTARD LAYER

1 pint fresh strawberries
  (about 2 cups)
2 envelopes Knox
  Unflavored Gelatine
½ cup cold milk
¾ cup milk, heated to
  boiling

½ cup sugar
4 eggs
1½ teaspoons vanilla
  extract
1 cup ice cubes (6 to 8)
1 cup (½ pint) heavy
  cream, whipped

Chop enough strawberries to equal 1 cup; halve lengthwise enough strawberries to equal ½ cup. Reserve remaining strawberries for garnish.

In a 5-cup blender container, sprinkle unflavored gelatine over cold milk; let stand 3 to 4 minutes. Add hot milk; cover and process at low speed 2 minutes. Add sugar, eggs, and vanilla. Add ice cubes, one at a time, and process at high speed until ice is melted. Pour into a large bowl; let stand until slightly thickened, about 5 minutes. Fold in whipped cream, then chopped strawberries.

On the strawberry layer, arrange halved strawberries, cut side out, against side of dish. Carefully spoon in cream 'n custard mixture. Chill until firm. Remove collar. Garnish with remaining strawberries.

DUTCH APPLE-CRUMB PIE   16 servings

- 2 9-inch graham cracker crumb crusts (recipe follows)
- 4 envelopes Knox Unflavored Gelatine
- ½ cup sugar, divided
- 4 eggs, separated
- 3 cups milk, divided
- 4 cups applesauce
- 1 teaspoon ground cinnamon
- ½ teaspoon ground nutmeg
- 1 can (20 ounces) unsweetened apple slices, drained and chopped

Make crumb crusts; chill.

In a large saucepan, mix unflavored gelatine with ¼ cup sugar. Beat egg yolks with 2 cups milk, blend into gelatine mixture. Stir over low heat until gelatine is completely dissolved and mixture thickens slightly, 5 to 8 minutes. Remove from heat; stir in remaining 1 cup milk, and the applesauce, cinnamon, and nutmeg. Chill, stirring occasionally, until mixture is the consistency of unbeaten egg whites.

In a medium bowl, beat egg whites until soft peaks form; gradually add remaining ¼ cup sugar and beat until stiff. Fold in gelatine mixture and apples. Divide mixture into prepared crumb crusts. Garnish each pie with ¼ cup reserved crumb mixture.

GRAHAM CRACKER CRUMB CRUST

- 2 cups graham cracker crumbs
- ½ cup finely chopped pecans
- ¼ cup soft butter or margarine
- 2 tablespoons sugar

In a small bowl, combine all ingredients. Reserve ½ cup of mixture; press remaining mixture into two 9-inch pie plates. Chill.

PARTY MINT TARTS

16 servings

2 envelopes Knox
  Unflavored Gelatine
1 cup sugar, divided
6 eggs, separated
1 cup water
1 cup green crème de
  menthe

2 cups (1 pint) heavy
  cream, whipped
16 purchased ready-to-use
  tart shells

In a small saucepan, mix unflavored gelatine with ½ cup sugar. Beat egg yolks with water; stir into gelatine mixture. Stir over low heat until gelatine is completely dissolved and mixture thickens slightly, 5 to 8 minutes. Remove from heat; stir in crème de menthe. Chill, stirring occasionally, until mixture mounds slightly when dropped from a spoon.

In a medium bowl, beat egg whites until soft peaks form; gradually add remaining ½ cup sugar and beat until stiff. Fold in gelatine mixture and whipped cream. Spoon into tart shells, piling filling high. Chill until set. 111 Decorate with whipped cream and chocolate curls, if desired.

PEACH MELBA CAKE

8 to 10 servings

1 can (16 ounces) sliced
  peaches
1 package (10 ounces)
  frozen raspberries,
  thawed
1 envelope Knox
  Unflavored Gelatine

1 cup (½ pint) heavy
  cream, whipped
8- or 9-inch angel food cake,
  cut into 1-inch cubes

Drain peaches and raspberries, reserving syrup from each. Cut peaches into chunks. Combine reserved syrups with enough water to equal 1½ cups.

In a medium saucepan, mix unflavored gelatine with ½ cup syrup mixture; stir over low heat until gelatine is completely dissolved. Remove from heat; add remaining 1 cup syrup mixture. Chill, stirring occasionally, until mixture is the consistency of unbeaten egg whites. Fold in whipped cream, cake cubes, peaches, and raspberries. Turn into an 8-cup mold; chill until firm.

Holiday happiness

At holiday time, you're busy. There are a thousand things to do, but not enough hours in the day to get them all accomplished. And yet you want holiday meals to be very special. Call on Knox Unflavored Gelatine to aid you in preparing magnificent holiday desserts at your convenience—they'll wait obligingly in the refrigerator for the big moment. You'll find here all the traditional flavors your family and guests love, to help you make any celebration merry.

HOLIDAY EGGNOG CHEER · 8 servings

This festive dessert has only 115 calories a serving, drops to 80 if you use artificial sweetener (equal to ¼ cup sugar)

1 envelope Knox Unflavored Gelatine	1½ cups milk
6 tablespoons sugar, divided	1 teaspoon brandy extract
4 eggs, separated	½ teaspoon rum extract
	½ teaspoon vanilla extract

In a medium saucepan, mix unflavored gelatine with 4 tablespoons sugar. Beat egg yolks with milk; blend into gelatine mixture, let stand 1 minute. Stir over low heat until gelatine is completely dissolved, about 5 minutes. Remove from heat; add brandy, rum, and vanilla extracts. Chill, stirring occasionally, until mixture mounds slightly when dropped from a spoon.

In a large bowl, beat egg whites until soft peaks form; gradually add remaining 2 tablespoons sugar and beat until stiff. Fold in gelatine mixture. Turn into 8 dessert dishes or a 4-cup bowl; chill until set. Sprinkle with ground nutmeg, if desired.

Great go-alongs: *Let this be the crowning delight of a delicious low-calorie holiday dinner. Start with tomato juice brightened with a squeeze of lemon, served with crisp celery and carrot sticks; go on to roast turkey (skip the gravy and stuffing), Slimmer's Cranberry Jelly (page 126), rutabagas mashed with orange juice, brussels sprouts lightly sprinkled with crushed cheese crackers, wedge of lettuce with Wish-Bone Low-Calorie Russian Dressing.*

JIFFY NESSELRODE DELIGHT

about 8 servings

2 envelopes Knox
    Unflavored Gelatine
½ cup cold water
1 cup boiling water
2 tablespoons sugar
2 cups (1 pint) vanilla ice
    cream, softened
1 teaspoon brandy extract

1 cup (½ pint) heavy
    cream, whipped
⅓ cup diced mixed candied
    fruit
⅓ cup small semisweet
    chocolate pieces
24 ladyfingers, split

In a large bowl, mix unflavored gelatine with cold water. Add boiling water and sugar and stir until gelatine is completely dissolved. Add ice cream and brandy extract and stir until ice cream is melted. Let stand until mixture mounds slightly when dropped from a spoon, about 7 minutes; fold in whipped cream, candied fruit, and chocolate pieces.

Line sides of a 1¾-quart soufflé dish or bowl with split ladyfingers. Carefully turn in gelatine mixture; chill until set, about 30 minutes.

Another way: *Substitute pound cake, cut into 1- x 2½-inch strips for the ladyfingers. Rum extract may be substituted for the brandy; or, if you prefer, substitute vanilla extract for a milder taste.*

CHAMPAGNE CRYSTAL BALL

8 to 12 servings

Just right for a New Year's Eve buffet or for open house the following day, perfect as the star of a wedding reception table

3 envelopes Knox
    Unflavored Gelatine
½ cup cold water
2½ cups boiling water

1 cup sugar
½ cup lemon juice
1½ cups (4/5 pint) cham-
    pagne or white wine

In a large bowl, mix unflavored gelatine with cold water. Add boiling water and sugar and stir until gelatine is completely dissolved. Stir in lemon juice. Cool. Add champagne, stirring gently to blend. Turn into a 1½-quart mold or bowl; chill until firm. Unmold to serve. If desired, garnish with whipped cream, surround with fresh flowers and green leaves.

FESTIVE CRANBERRY PIE   8 servings

2 envelopes Knox
   Unflavored Gelatine
1/3 cup sugar
1 1/2 cups orange juice,
   divided

1 jar (14 ounces) cranberry-
   orange relish
1/2 cup chopped walnuts
9-inch graham cracker
   crust*

In a medium saucepan, mix unflavored gelatine with sugar; add 3/4 cup orange juice. Let stand 1 minute. Stir over medium heat until gelatine is completely dissolved, about 3 minutes. Remove from heat; add remaining 3/4 cup orange juice. Chill, stirring occasionally, until mixture is the consistency of unbeaten egg whites.

Fold in relish and walnuts. Turn into prepared crust; chill until firm. Garnish with whipped topping and walnut halves, if desired.

*See recipe on page 109; use half of each ingredient for one 9-inch crust.

114 ORANGE-CRANBERRY   6 servings
CHIFFON PIE

Glorious flavor, holiday color, airy texture—here's the perfect dessert to top off, sweetly but lightly, a classic (but very filling) feast on Thanksgiving or Christmas

1 envelope Knox
   Unflavored Gelatine
1/2 cup orange juice
1 can (1 pound) whole
   cranberry sauce

1 tablespoon grated
   orange peel
2 egg whites
1/4 cup sugar
1 8-inch crumb crust

In a medium saucepan, mix gelatine with orange juice. Let stand 1 minute. Add cranberry sauce. Stir over low heat until gelatine is completely dissolved and cranberries are broken up and heated, about 3 minutes. Remove from heat; add orange peel. Chill, stirring occasionally, until mixture is the consistency of unbeaten egg whites.

In a medium bowl, beat egg whites until soft peaks form; gradually add sugar and beat until stiff. Fold in gelatine mixture. Turn into prepared crust. Chill until firm. Garnish with whipped cream and grated orange peel, if desired.

PUMPKIN CHIFFON PIE

8 servings

Lighter, less filling than grandma's, but every bit as good (maybe better, if that isn't heresy), this favorite-flavor pie will grace any holiday meal

1 envelope Knox Unflavored Gelatine	½ teaspoon ginger
¾ cup light brown sugar, divided	¾ cup evaporated milk or whole milk
1½ teaspoons cinnamon	3 eggs, separated
½ teaspoon nutmeg	1¼ cups canned pumpkin
	Baked 9-inch pastry shell

In a medium saucepan, combine unflavored gelatine, ½ cup of the brown sugar, the cinnamon, nutmeg, and ginger. Stir in evaporated milk and egg yolks; blend well. Let stand 1 minute. Stir over low heat and cook until gelatine is completely dissolved and mixture thickens slightly, 5 to 7 minutes. Remove from heat; stir in pumpkin. Chill, stirring occasionally, until mixture mounds slightly when dropped from a spoon.

In a medium bowl, beat egg whites until soft peaks form; gradually add remaining ¼ cup brown sugar and beat until stiff. Fold in pumpkin mixture. Turn into pastry shell; chill until firm. Garnish with whipped cream, if desired.

PUMPKIN RIBBON PIE

8 servings

Pumpkin pie is such a favorite during the fall and winter, you'll welcome this new way to make it—two traditionally spicy pumpkin layers encase a fluffy, creamy center strip

1 envelope Knox Unflavored Gelatine	¾ cup canned pumpkin
¾ cup sugar, divided	½ teaspoon cinnamon
2 eggs, separated	¼ teaspoon nutmeg
1 cup milk	¼ teaspoon ground cloves
½ teaspoon vanilla extract	Baked 9-inch pastry shell
2 packages (3 ounces each) cream cheese, softened	

In a medium saucepan, mix unflavored gelatine with ½ cup sugar. Beat egg yolks with milk; stir into gelatine mixture; let stand 1 minute. Stir over low heat until gelatine is completely dissolved, about 5 minutes. Remove from heat; add vanilla. In a large bowl, beat cream cheese until smooth; gradually beat in gelatine mixture. Chill, stirring occasionally, until mixture mounds slightly when dropped from a spoon.

In a medium bowl, beat egg whites until soft peaks form; gradually add remaining ¼ cup sugar and beat until stiff. Fold in cheese mixture.

Reserve 1 cup cheese mixture. To remaining mixture, fold in pumpkin mixed with cinnamon, nutmeg, and cloves. Turn half the pumpkin mixture into pastry shell. Spread on reserved cheese mixture; top with remaining pumpkin mixture. Chill until firm.

MINCEMEAT CREME PIE 8 servings

Welcome a new version of old-fashioned mince pie—one that's lighter, with a creamy filling spiked with fresh orange for added flavor

2 envelopes Knox
   Unflavored Gelatine
½ cup cold milk
½ cup milk, heated to
   boiling
2 eggs
½ orange, cut up and
   seeded
⅓ cup sugar

1 cup (½ pint) heavy
   cream
6 ice cubes (about 1 cup)
1½ cups prepared
   mincemeat
9-inch graham cracker
   crust* or baked
   pastry shell

In a 5-cup blender container, sprinkle unflavored gelatine over cold milk; let stand 3 to 4 minutes. Add hot milk; cover and process at low speed until gelatine is completely dissolved, about 2 minutes. Add eggs, orange, and sugar; cover and process at high speed until orange is finely chopped. Add cream. Add ice cubes, one at a time, and process until ice is melted. Add mincemeat and process at high speed, turning on and off, until chopped.

Turn into prepared crust; chill until firm.

*See recipe on page 109; use half of each ingredient for one 9-inch crust.

CUPID'S CHERRY PIE

8 servings

Make this delicious, delicately pink dessert for Valentine's Day, for a shower or a birthday party—for any occasion when you want to create something with which to say "I love you"

- 1 envelope Knox Unflavored Gelatine
- 6 tablespoons sugar, divided
- 2 eggs, separated
- 1¼ cups milk, divided
- ¼ cup maraschino cherry syrup
- ¼ teaspoon almond extract or ½ teaspoon vanilla

- 3 drops red food coloring
- 1 package (8 ounces) cream cheese, softened
- ¼ cup chopped maraschino cherries
- 9-inch graham cracker crust*

In a medium saucepan, mix unflavored gelatine with 4 tablespoons sugar. Beat egg yolks with ½ cup milk; blend into gelatine mixture. Let stand 1 minute. Stir over low heat until gelatine is completely dissolved, about 5 minutes. Remove from heat; stir in remaining ¾ cup milk, cherry syrup, almond extract, and food coloring. In a medium bowl, beat cream cheese until smooth. Gradually beat in gelatine mixture. Chill, stirring occasionally, until mixture mounds slightly when dropped from a spoon.

In a medium bowl, beat egg whites until soft peaks form; gradually add remaining 2 tablespoons sugar and beat until stiff. Fold in gelatine mixture and cherries. Turn into prepared crust; chill until firm. Garnish with additional maraschino cherries, if desired.

*See recipe on page 109; use half of each ingredient for one 9-inch crust.

118

IRISH COFFEE PIE

8 servings

St. Patrick's Day comes only once a year, not nearly often enough to serve this great cream/coffee/whiskey pie with its subtle flavor, its piled-high good looks!

2 envelopes Knox Unflavored Gelatine
6 tablespoons sugar, divided
3 eggs, separated
2 cups cold strong coffee
2 cups (1 pint) coffee ice cream, softened

⅓ cup Irish whiskey
Baked 9-inch pastry shell
2 cups (1 pint) sweetened whipped cream or whipped topping
Grated semisweet chocolate

In a medium saucepan, mix unflavored gelatine with 5 tablespoons sugar. Beat egg yolks with coffee; blend into gelatine mixture. Let stand 1 minute. Stir over low heat until gelatine is completely dissolved, about 5 minutes. Remove from heat; add ice cream, stirring until melted; stir in whiskey. Chill, stirring occasionally, until mixture mounds slightly when dropped from a spoon.

In a small bowl, beat egg whites until soft peaks form; gradually add remaining 1 tablespoon sugar and beat until stiff. Fold in gelatine mixture. Turn into pastry shell; chill until firm. Garnish with whipped cream and grated chocolate.

The great jams and jellies revolution

When you spread jam on your morning toast or jelly on biscuits, you probably think about making jams and jellies at home. But it's a big nuisance, isn't it—all that peeling and cutting up and chopping, all the careful timing, the long cooking, the straining, dripping, and even after all that, sometimes the jelly doesn't gel. Homemade jams and jellies are loaded with calories anyway, aren't they? Wrong, all wrong. There's a new and better way, the unflavored gelatine way. Easy. Sure-fire results. Best of all, only 10 to 30 calories per tablespoon, as against the 60 or so calories of jams and jellies made the conventional way.

Using Knox Unflavored Gelatine reduces the large amounts of sugar usually required in making jams and jellies at home. It eliminates long cooking times, too.

Most fruits have ample natural sweetness—all the sugar that recipes call for is not only for sweetening, but to help make the jelly gel, the jam thicken. Knox takes care of that problem, producing easy, good-flavored gels with little cooking, little sugar. Indeed, they can be made entirely without sugar—the recipes that follow have been developed using sugar but you can, if you like, use equivalent amounts of artificial sweetener if you're on a special diet.

Another advantage is that jars of these new-way jams and jellies need not be sealed with paraffin. They are stored short-term in the refrigerator or long-term in the freezer, ready whenever you want them.

First, the background on this new bread-spread technique. Then try one of the easy recipes. Once you've proved to yourself how easy it is, how excellent the results are, you'll want to try them all and go on to invent new flavor combinations.

Fruit

Fresh fruit should be firm, ripe, and unblemished for optimum color and flavor.

Canned fruit may be diet-packed (that is, in water) or packed in light or heavy syrup—just bear in mind that the heavier the syrup the more calories it contains; it's sugar that makes the syrup heavy and the calories mount up.

Fruit juices should be unsweetened to avoid excess calories. Otherwise, let your imagination have full play. You can even make, by the unflavored-gelatine method, jellies you don't usually find in stores—orange, for example. You can work out ways to make jellies with fruit nectar—even with prune juice, if that idea intrigues you. Just avoid fresh or frozen pineapple juice (canned is fine) and you'll be successful.

Sweetening

Granulated sugar works best. Brown sugar does not gel well. Honey may be used instead of a part of the granulated sugar, in proportions of 25 percent honey to 75 percent sugar.

If you wish to use a sugar substitute, the approach is a little different. Omit the sugar in the recipe and cook as directed. When the cooking is complete, stir in a sugar substitute equivalent to the amount of sugar the recipe calls for.

Containers

Use small jars, 4- to 8-ounce capacity. Though you needn't seal the jars with paraffin, they should have tight-fitting covers. Date and label each container so that you'll be certain of the contents, and so that you'll use up the oldest first.

Storage

Along with all their other advantages, these jams and jellies keep well. For a short time (up to 4 weeks), they can be stored in the refrigerator. For a long period (up to 1 year), they should be stored in the freezer.

Now try the recipes, and enjoy the sweet results.

Opposite: Grape Jelly, Peach and Strawberry Jams (recipes on page 124)

APPLE JELLY
about 2½ cups

Good, old-time flavor, and only 10 calories per tablespoon

1 envelope Knox	**¼ cup sugar**
Unflavored Gelatine	**2½ cups apple juice**

In a medium saucepan, mix unflavored gelatine and sugar. Blend in apple juice. Stir over low heat until gelatine is completely dissolved, about 3 minutes.

Ladle into jars. Cover and cool slightly before refrigerating.

Another way: *For Applemint Jelly, stir in ½ teaspoon peppermint extract and, if desired, a few drops of green food coloring after cooking is completed.*

GRAPE JELLY
about 2½ cups

Like grandma used to make, but it took her hours—this is the jiffy way, and only 15 calories in each tablespoon

122

1 envelope Knox	**2½ cups unsweetened**
Unflavored Gelatine	**grape juice**
¼ cup sugar	

In a medium saucepan, mix unflavored gelatine with sugar. Blend in grape juice. Stir over low heat until gelatine is completely dissolved, about 3 minutes.
Ladle into jars. Cover and cool slightly before refrigerating.

Other ways: *Use the conventional purple grape juice for this, or vary by using the newer red or white grape juices.*

PEACH JAM

about 3 cups

(Illustration page 123)

A peach of a sweet at only 10 calories per tablespoon!

5 cups sliced peeled peaches (about 2½ pounds)	1 tablespoon lemon juice
	1 envelope Knox Unflavored Gelatine
⅓ cup sugar	¼ cup cold water

In a medium saucepan, combine peaches, sugar, and lemon juice. Heat 5 minutes, crushing peaches slightly. Bring to a boil; boil rapidly, stirring constantly, 1 minute.

In a small bowl, sprinkle unflavored gelatine over water. Let stand 1 minute. Add to peach mixture and heat, stirring until gelatine is dissolved, about 3 minutes.

Let jam stand 5 minutes, skimming off foam with a spoon. Ladle into jars. Cover and cool slightly before refrigerating.

124

STRAWBERRY JAM

about 2 cups

(Illustration page 123)

Because it cooks so briefly, this tastes more like the fresh fruit than most strawberry jams—and it contains only 15 calories per tablespoon

4 cups sliced strawberries (about 2 pints)	1 envelope Knox Unflavored Gelatine
⅓ cup sugar	½ cup cold water
2 tablespoons lemon juice	

In a medium saucepan, combine strawberries, sugar, and lemon juice. Heat 5 minutes, crushing berries slightly. Bring to a boil; boil rapidly, stirring constantly, 3 minutes.

In a small bowl, sprinkle unflavored gelatine over cold water. Let stand 1 minute. Add to strawberry mixture and heat, stirring until gelatine is completely dissolved, about 3 minutes.

Let jam stand 5 minutes, skimming off foam with a spoon. Ladle into jars. Cover and cool slightly before refrigerating.

APRICOT JAM

about 2 cups

Here's the ultimate easy jam—no preliminary preparation of fruit, you don't have to wait until apricots come in season, and it contains only 30 calories per tablespoon

2 cans (17 ounces each)
   apricot halves
1 envelope Knox
   Unflavored Gelatine

2 tablespoons sugar
Water

Drain apricots, reserving liquid. In a 5-cup blender container, purée apricots.

In a medium saucepan, mix unflavored gelatine and sugar. To reserved liquid, add water to make 1 cup; blend into gelatine mixture. Stir over low heat until gelatine is completely dissolved, about 3 minutes. Stir in puréed apricots.

Ladle into jars. Cover; cool slightly before refrigerating.

Another way: *For Spicy Apricot Jam, add ½ teaspoon ground nutmeg to the gelatine and sugar.*

BLUEBERRY JAM

about 4 cups

Tang of orange juice and peel gives this jam a fresh, new flavor —"costs" only 10 calories per tablespoon

4 cups blueberries
   (about 2 pints)
¼ cup sugar
¼ teaspoon grated orange
   peel

1 envelope Knox
   Unflavored Gelatine
¼ cup orange juice

In a medium saucepan, combine blueberries, sugar, and orange peel. Heat 5 minutes, crushing berries slightly. Bring to a boil; boil rapidly, stirring constantly, 1 minute.

In a small bowl, sprinkle unflavored gelatine over orange juice. Let stand 1 minute. Add to blueberry mixture and heat, stirring until gelatine is completely dissolved, about 3 minutes.

Let jam stand 5 minutes, skimming off foam with a spoon. Ladle into jars. Cover and cool slightly before refrigerating.

SLIMMER'S CRANBERRY JELLY

about 4 cups

Cranberry jelly, to many people a must at holidays such as Thanksgiving and Christmas, and enjoyed throughout the year, is one of those little extras that weight-loss dieters hate to do without. Regular-recipe homemade or canned cranberry jelly averages about 100 calories for a ¼-cup serving. The version below cuts the figure to only about 15 calories for the same portion

2 envelopes Knox Unflavored Gelatine	3¼ cups low-calorie cranberry juice cocktail, heated to boiling
½ cup cold low-calorie cranberry juice cocktail	

In a medium bowl, mix unflavored gelatine with cold cranberry juice. Add hot cranberry juice; stir until gelatine is completely dissolved. Turn into a 4-cup bowl or mold; chill until firm. Unmold to serve.

Storage: *Slimmer's Cranberry Jelly is so super easy, you can make it fresh (cut the recipe in half, if you like) each time you wish to serve it. Refrigerate up to 5 days. Do not freeze this jelly; it will crystallize.*

Index

127